James Burstall is a thoughtful, constructive and strategic leader and in this book there is a rich series of insights. Leaders from every industry will find this an invaluable tool. I thoroughly recommend it.
Gloria Hunniford OBE, Television and radio presenter

James Burstall is a natural storyteller and, boy, has he got a great story to tell. Written with wit and warmth, *The Flexible Method* is full of revealing anecdotes to illustrate that even the most catastrophic change brings opportunity if you face it with the right attitude.
Katy Thorogood, Chief Creative Officer, True North Productions

Great leaders share their secrets and James Burstall reveals all. Cataclysms are unpredictable, but surviving them in the future shouldn't be.
Kevin Maguire, *Daily Mirror* and *New Statesman*

Deciphering the code and distilling its essence is where James Burstall has excelled here. His curiosity and interrogative skills unlock many insights into the acquisition and application of leadership skills – a revealing and uplifting work.
Dermot Murnaghan, Award-winning host, *Sky News Tonight*

Burstall's most important message will surprise some: to protect your revenues, you need to hold onto your values and put your people first. James Burstall is preparing for the next global disaster now. We would all be wise to do the same.
Dorothy Byrne, President, Murray Edwards College, University of Cambridge; Former Head of News and Current Affairs, Channel 4

I simply love this book. It prepares you for the worst crisis and helps you get through it leaner and stronger. This book is like a business bible. Usually founders/CEOs are either very creative or amazing at growing a business. It is rare when someone is excellent at both. James is one of the rare.
Tony Kitous, Founder, Comptoir Libanais Group Plc

This is a timely and important book for all types of leaders. James has brought deep wisdom from his own experience and a diverse set of leaders to think about the crises of our times. It is a critical tool kit for leaders who plan to thrive through these times and seize the opportunities that are inherent within them.
Dr Andrew White, Director of the Advanced, Management and Leadership Programme, Saïd Business School, University of Oxford

Forged in the competitive and demanding world of TV production, James Burstall has emerged as one of the most astute, dynamic and creative leaders in the industry. His experience, coupled with a deep connection with his people, has produced a book of merit and insight.
John McVay OBE, Chief Executive, PACT, Producers Alliance for Cinema and Television

In the ocean of same-same business books out there, James's unique experience, and voice, make this a stand-out fabulous read.

Nigel Marsh, author, _Fat, Forty and Fired_; founder of Sydney Skinny; former CEO of Leo Burnett Advertising

This is a cracking read for anybody leading a team or running a business. James is a smart, kind and humble business leader and his insights are invaluable. I shall be keeping this book to hand as it will be a useful tool for the future.

Donna Suarez, Publisher, _Celebrity Magazine_

Unpredictable futures call for unshakeable truths. I found in _The Flexible Method_ an insightful, confident, bold and refreshingly articulate affirmation of leadership values that get out from behind the desk and into the lived reality of a crisis. Put simply, this is what works, so do this!

Stuart Chatterton, Safeguarding Manager, Capital City College Group

Publilius Syrus said, 'Anyone can take the tiller when the sea is calm.' James's experiences and research identify the essential qualities and functions of an inspirational leader that will ensure organizational resilience in any crisis.

David Hudson MBE, military and business leadership coach and mentor

James shares his creative use of 'the Flexible Method' within his global business in this inspiring book. Equally appropriate to large international corporations through to small family-owned enterprises, his 'Flexible Method' offers a constructive checklist to consider. No wonder the Argonon Group is prospering!

James Ryeland FICS, Managing Director, George Hammond Marine Ltd

The book is just what is needed now, as we emerge from one tsunami and face at least two more on the horizon. Those responsible for risk planning will find it a very useful tool not only to re-evaluate their own plans but also possibly to refocus them, adopting the flexible principles. A great read.

Robert Neill, international lawyer, Herbert Smith Freehills

James was listed in 'Kindness & Leadership 50 Leading Lights 2021' because he has demonstrated over many years his ability to lead an ambitious, creative business whilst holding onto the core values of empathy, diversity and inclusion. In this book, we see that these values are a key driver to success in the midst of a crisis. It is an invaluable tool for business leaders from all backgrounds.

Pinky Lilani CBE, founder, Women of the Future Network

Post-Covid leadership is no longer about driving profit for shareholders, against all odds. Now, more than ever before, the global workforce is gravitating toward purpose-driven businesses run by enlightened leaders who truly live by their values. James Burstall shares vital insights and practical techniques that will inspire leaders from all sectors, based on real-life experience, against a backdrop of entertaining stories from the world of television production, and more. _The Flexible Method_ is essential reading for all CEOs, entrepreneurs and leaders.

Sarah Shields, founder, Thrive Executive Search

The Flexible Method is a first-of-its-kind book that offers leadership lessons for thriving in our crises-ridden world! Award-winning CEO and author of this book James Burstall, along with his team, has demonstrated resilience and agility in steering a group of business organizations through unprecedented emergencies during recent times. This masterpiece of writing is a must-read for mastering the art and science of leading in a disruptive world.

Professor Lalit Johri, Senior Fellow in International Business, University of Oxford

We're not prepared. But the good news is, we can be. Thankfully, James Burstall, CEO of entertainment powerhouse Argonon, has created something unique: a business book that is filled with specific actions we can take today to protect and grow our business.

Seth G. Sherman, Co-President, Parabolic Content, LLC

The Flexible Method is a tool we all can use to prepare for the inevitable ... a crisis that needs quick and thoughtful management. A book that shows us what we thought we knew but didn't and how to correct course before the disaster strikes.

Edward McDonnell, award-winning producer, *Sicario, Robin Hood, Eagle Eye*

Jam-packed with brilliant ideas on how to cope with a catastrophe, both professionally and personally, this book should be read by everyone running a business today. The easy-to-read, practical takeaways on his flexible approach to business management are top-class.

Chantal Rickards, former Chair BAFTA

James's commitment to growing his business, the Argonon group, his bravery, commitment and dedication to the content space, will make this book a must-read for anyone wishing to follow in his steps.

Thomas Dey, President and Chief Executive Officer, ACF Investment Bank

James Burstall is a true humanist who knows how to put all the inexhaustible qualities and hidden strengths of a team at the service of business. James understands that a company is first and foremost a human collective that alone provides the adaptability and flexibility needed to turn adversity into strength.

Mathias Dosne, CEO Nautilus Food Group

This book is of relevance to anyone in a leadership role who wants to understand what it takes to lead a team successfully through challenge and enable an organization to survive and then thrive. It captures the essence and skills of good and practical leadership in a manner that makes one reflect on how you can be a better leader.

Paul Jaques, Lieutenant General, British Army

James has a solutions-based mindset, embraces change and knows it's critical to growth and success. And he feels that healthy people equal a healthy company. He's always been a forward-thinking executive and I can't think of a better person to write this book in today's climate, since he has been living the Flexible Method for years.

Renee Hauch, principal at JM Search

If this challenging world is teaching us anything, it's to try to find 'nuances' in our decisions. *The Flexible Method* is about those nuances James Burstall gathered in his rich experience: they help us find the creativity to constantly adapt and take the necessary risks, while also taking care of people. It's about giving both our company and our team a better chance to thrive in a healthy way.
Nathalie Wogue, Wogue Entertainment

James Burstall is one of the British TV sector's outstanding entrepreneurs, building a successful and truly independent production business during a period of both huge opportunity and unprecedented challenges. Argonon has married organic growth with clever acquisitions and James has navigated its growth for more than a decade.
Chris Curtis, Editor, *Broadcast*

Establishing, growing and steering a successful business of scale through multiple crises not only demonstrates James' smart business acumen but reveals the wisdom of a first-class leader.
Miles Jarvis, Managing Director, Phoenix Television

James Burstall's story demonstrates that unlocking our creativity, doggedly pursuing purpose and protecting your core values, especially at times of crisis, is the key to flexible, mission-orientated leadership.
Caroline Norbury, OBE, Chief Executive, Creative UK

The Flexible Method reflects the brilliant abilities and multicultural life philosophy of James Burstall, which can be summed up in a powerful motto: 'Dare! Care! Share!' Following the steps laid out in this book will be highly effective for readers to maximize success in business as well as in their personal lives.
Professor Doctor Esra Ekmekçi, Professor of Law, University of Istanbul, and Founder, Dream Factory

James Burstall's *The Flexible Method* provides readers with a well-organized toolbox containing a coherent set of guidelines and actions for managing crises. As an owner of a small business, I found that the many real-life examples aptly illustrate how the Flexible Method principles can apply to one's business regardless of its size.
Richard Louis, CEO, FitSpace Gyms

James Burstall is both a major league content creator in his own right, plus a successful transatlantic business founder in one of the hardest industries to consistently conquer: TV. He has done this through a combination of great ideas, talent management and empathy. *The Flexible Method* describes his approach in helpful and well-illustrated detail. It is therefore invaluable for anyone looking to build a business, whether in media or any other industry.
Professor Alex Connock, Exeter University, Head of Creative Business, National Film & Television School

When pandemic pandemonium erupted in 2019, for many panic ensued, followed in short order by paralysis and despair. Not James Burstall. After a deep breath and short period of reflection, he swung into action, armed with a powerful strategy developed during the 2008 financial crisis. Using this 'Flexible Method', his company not only became the first TV company to return to filming but took care its people thrived. This hands-on, how-to book shows exactly how James and his team did that, with profound and actionable lessons for us all.
Bill Brand, actor, writer and leadership consultant

In *The Flexible Method* James Burstall illustrates compellingly and eloquently how the 'up-set' can truly lead to the 'set-up' for growth through harnessing the right blend of culture, resources and attitude. An eminently readable 'must-read'.
Giles Watkins, author of *Positive Sleep*, former MD Shell, Asia Pacific

James is a trailblazing and dynamic leading light in the independent television sector. He was one of the first CEOs in the business who understood how to formalize diversity and hardwire it into his business. As a result he showed the sector just how commercially successful as well as culturally rewarding recruiting and developing a diverse workforce is. And beyond that he understands the value of having a healthy work culture in an industry not always known for this. I can't think of anyone better placed to write about leadership.
Lucy Pilkington, Managing Director, Milk and Honey Productions

James Burstall has created an exceptional guide to preparing, managing and leading through crises to get to the best possible result. *The Flexible Method* moved me with its practical, personal insights and examples that teach in an impactful and memorable way. It is essential reading for leaders across all industries.
Steve Arikian, former Chairman and CEO, Genesis Research

The Flexible Method is a fantastic look into how resilience can help you through the hardest of times. Overflowing with terrific tips and tricks to help you come out on top, is both incredibly useful and filled with fun.
Paul Boross, speaker, author and host of The Humourology Podcast

Struggling to keep your head and make good decisions in the unpredictable world of modern leadership, where the only certainty is further uncertainty, then *The Flexible Method* is for you. James shares his insights of running innovative creative companies, and this book shows that you don't need to compromise your core values in times of crisis, rather you need to hang onto them even more firmly.
Ade Rawcliffe, Group Director of Diversity and Inclusion, ITV Global Networks

The Flexible Method

*Prepare to Prosper in the
Next Global Crisis*

JAMES BURSTALL

NICHOLAS BREALEY
PUBLISHING

London • Boston

First published by Nicholas Brealey Publishing in 2023
An imprint of John Murray Press
A division of Hodder & Stoughton Ltd,
An Hachette UK company

1

A CIP catalogue record for this title is available from the British Library

Trade Paperback ISBN 978 1 39980 6 527
eBook ISBN 978 1 39980 6 558
Argonon Edition ISBN 978 1 39981 0 890

Typeset by KnowledgeWorks Global Ltd.

Printed and bound in Great Britain by Clays Ltd, Elcograf S.p.A.

John Murray Press policy is to use papers that are natural, renewable and recyclable
products and made from wood grown in sustainable forests. The logging and manufacturing
processes are expected to conform to the environmental regulations of the country of origin.

John Murray Press
Carmelite House
50 Victoria Embankment
London EC4Y 0DZ

Nicholas Brealey Publishing
Hachette Book Group
Market Place, Center 53, State Street
Boston, MA 02109, USA

www.nicholasbrealey.com

For John

About the Author

Photo by Andy Sillett

James Burstall is CEO of Argonon, one of the world's top international independent production groups. The group is headquartered in London with hubs in New York, Los Angeles, Liverpool and Glasgow.

Argonon has won more than 125 international awards, including Emmys, BAFTAs and Royal Television Society Awards.

Founded by Burstall in 2011, Argonon encompasses nine production companies. The group produces and distributes content across drama, documentary, investigative current affairs, science, tech, reality, lifestyle, gameshow, prime time entertainment and branded content. Their biggest hits include *The Masked Singer, House Hunters International, Worzel Gummidge, Hard Cell, Cash in the Attic, Dispatches* and *Mysteries of the Abandoned.*

The group work with top talent including Rita Ora, Davina McCall, Mo Gilligan, Joel Dommett, Jonathan Ross, David Attenborough, Robin Thicke, Ne-Yo, Vanessa Redgrave, Catherine Tate, Mackenzie Crook, Joss Stone, Kelis, Sharon and Kelly Osbourne, Snoop Dog and many more.

Prior to forming Argonon, Burstall was CEO of Leopard Films. During his ten-year tenure, the company produced long-running series and formats including *Cash in the Attic*, which has aired in 167 countries, as well as award-winning documentary series, and the dramas *Eve* (RTS winner), *Missing* and *An Englishman in New York*, starring John Hurt and Cynthia Nixon. Burstall has won commendations in the House of Commons and the US Senate.

Before Leopard Films, Burstall worked as an executive producer and producer-director for broadcasters all over the world. Prior to his television career, he was a journalist, working as a writer and editor in Paris, London and New York for *Vanity Fair, Condé Nast Traveler, HG, Vogue*, the *Daily Mail* and the *Evening Standard*.

Burstall has studied at the business schools of the University of Oxford and Stanford Graduate School in California. He is a speaker at Saïd Business School, University of Oxford, on entrepreneurship and ethical leadership and has recently contributed a chapter to a book on how diversity and inclusion give business the cutting edge. He was selected as one of the Top 50 Leading Lights, Kindness & Leadership, 2021, and in 2022 received a special tribute for Disruption, Innovation and Creativity from PACT, the Producers Alliance for Cinema and Television.

Argonon's pioneering Covid-19 protocols enabled production to start up during the pandemic and have been widely shared throughout the industry.

Contents

Introduction

We live in an uncertain world where health emergencies, war, cost of living crises, political and social unrest, disruptive technology and climate change are now a fact of life. I am no doom-monger but it is clear the next global crisis is just around the corner. This means the time to prepare yourself, your team and your organization is now.

Fear not. This is an optimistic book.

The Flexible Method shows what you can do to future-proof your organization against the next crisis. It comprises a set of practical tools that distils hard-won experience into a hands-on guide to ensure you not only survive the next crisis but thrive.

It is tried and tested. And it works.

Although partly set in my industry, the world of entertainment, this book contains tools that anyone can use and which are transferable to any sector.

I run one of the world's leading independent production groups called Argonon. We have won more than 125 international awards and produce shows for Netflix, the BBC, ITV, Discovery, Snapchat and many other broadcasters around the world. You may have heard of *The Masked Singer, Worzel Gummidge, Hard Cell, Mysteries of the Abandoned* and *Cash in the Attic*. They're our shows.

I had thought that 2020 was going to be our year. A year for getting 2020 vision on life and the world, for getting my business to a new place, perhaps gaining some valuable insights in my own life. Yet on 10 March 2020, we closed the front doors of our offices in London, New York, LA, Liverpool and Glasgow. We sent everyone home. The spread of Covid-19 across the world meant that pretty much all work had ceased. We were told no production could safely take place for weeks or even months.

The TV industry was particularly badly hit by Covid. All production was halted overnight, leaving hundreds of thousands of media professionals facing ruin. We never expected a global pandemic to come along and obliterate the world as we knew it.

This was an existential threat. If we don't film, we don't make money, and so we can't pay our bills. My partner and I drove to our house in Kent and locked the door. It was dark and raining. Outside, everything was eerily silent. Sitting there at home, I wondered how I could have got things so wrong.

To be honest, I was terrified. I had no idea what was happening to us and was genuinely fearful for our lives. I also thought my beloved company, which I had built over 20 years, might go under. I felt guilty – I had failed my partner, my team, my family and friends, myself. It was beyond me how things could get this bad, so suddenly.

I was not alone. Whatever industry you are in, I'm sure you also vividly recall the fear and uncertainty of that time.

We did take a hit from Covid. We came out of the pandemic with a 9 per cent fall in revenue, but this was compared to an industry average of 19 per cent. Our major competitor suffered a whopping 30 per cent drop.

After initially furloughing staff, we actually increased our headcount during Covid, and our revenues are now up 50 per cent year-on-year, making us the fastest growing independent production group of our size.

Our company is leaner but not meaner. It has evolved and is prospering. Not despite the global crisis but because of it. How can this be?

We had one invaluable advantage – the Flexible Method. It was first developed by Argonon during another existential crisis, the 2008 Credit Crunch. Born in a crisis and refined over many more, it proved so successful during the pandemic that I am now sharing it to help other leaders.

I appreciate you giving up your precious time to read this book – I know how busy you are. I do not take up your schedule lightly. I have a responsibility to make it worth your while.

This set of working tools is not a dry list of things to do; it is a personal book full of heartening stories from a wide range of people who put elements of the Flexible Method into action. It changed their lives for the better. I am convinced it will also change yours.

The Flexible Method can not only save your organization money, it can also develop your skills as a powerful and effective leader. It will change the way you approach problems using critical thinking.

It also helps counter another modern scourge: stress and anxiety. It can make you healthier in mind and body and give you confidence to cope with whatever the future holds.

None of the Flexible Method is easy, but I will take you through it one step at a time. I encourage you to try it. I truly believe that you can transform your future by reading this book and putting it into action.

You may ask with scepticism why someone from the entertainment industry could possibly be qualified to give you advice. Some people think the creative industries are just a nice add-on but ultimately irrelevant to business. I'd like to set the record straight. We bring in more money in the UK than life sciences, the aeronautical and automotive industries, oil and gas combined, accounting for 7 per cent of gross value added (GVA), which provides a dollar value for the amount of goods and services that have been produced in a country, minus the impact of subsidies and taxes. Seven per cent, dare I say, is huge, contributing £116 billion annually to the UK economy, that is US$140 billion.

In the US, the creative industries represent 5 per cent of GVA. Also a significant number. This equates to $877 billion, not including the digital economy. What's more, the creative industries are major creators of employment. We employ 2.1 million people in Great Britain and 9 million people in the US.

So why is this sector a useful case study? The independent TV production industry is expert at managing tight margins. We have to be on top of cost control. We have learned to be nimble, always ready to pivot. This makes an independent TV production company an excellent template for crisis management because other industries are going to have to adopt similar ways of thinking that are perhaps not currently in their DNA.

A good example of how this way of thinking stood us in good stead was *The Masked Singer*, the crazy studio singing show we produce for ITV where celebrity guests perform hit songs dressed in giant masks, such as Queen Bee, Duck or Badger. A celebrity panel, along with the audience, try to guess their identity simply by listening to their voices.

We were able to restart shooting shows such as this during the pandemic thanks to the pioneering Covid protocols we set in motion, putting a gazillion measures in place to make sure our people were safe. Celebrity panelist Davina McCall's first show in the middle of 2020 was in an eerily empty studio. Instead of a noisy studio audience of hundreds, she, host Joel Dommett and the other celebrity judges, singer Rita Ora and comedians Mo Gilligan and Jonathan Ross, performed to an empty room in front of a handful of masked camera crew. The panel were separated from each other by Perspex screens.

Davina recalls:

'It was jarring. At first, we couldn't hear each other and it was a bit odd. And then we worked with it. We'd touch the glass, we'd look at each other, we'd make a joke out of not being able to hear.

At that stage we decided not to pretend this isn't happening. It's happening to everybody at home. It's happening to everybody at work. Make a joke out of it. Talk about it, laugh about it. Everybody understands. We found it weird at the beginning, but two days in, we didn't find it weird anymore. It just became how we worked.

'If something amazing was happening, Rita and I used to both put our hands against each other's on the screen. We acclimatized to a new normal with an unbelievable speed. It was actually one of the best shows we ever did.'

Davina and the other stars of *The Masked Singer* pivoted, took the new situation in their stride and turned what could have been a debilitating impediment into a triumph.

Meanwhile, in the US, 19-year-old entertainer and rising Instagram celebrity La'Ron Hines had just moved from Mississippi to Hollywood to launch a showbiz career supported by his mentor, the singer-songwriter Robin Thicke. His future looked promising. Then Covid-19 struck. Auditions dried up, the industry shut down, so he moved back home where his mother insisted he made himself useful working at her daycare centre.

Initially horrified at the prospect of giving up a performer's life for a childcare job, La'Ron instead seized the day. He adapted to the circumstances, saw an opportunity and started producing a series of funny videos of the kids on TikTok called *Are You Smarter than a Preschooler?*. It went viral overnight. Within a few months, La'Ron attracted the attention of Beyoncé Knowles, comedians Tina Fey and Amy Poehler, and ended up back in Hollywood at the Golden Globes.

La'Ron and Davina tell their stories later in the book, along with leaders from a wide range of sectors, including retail, hospitality, legal, travel, culture, fitness, sailing, politics and farming. They all share valuable insights into how they dealt with crises.

Their stories will help you become more flexible and agile in your own thinking and hone your response to crises. They reveal the thinking processes and logic behind their decision-making.

The Flexible Method will show you the precise steps you need to take to put flexible thinking into practice. It is designed to help you prepare for the next big crisis and come out on top. I have written it to give you hope. Things can get bad, but there is always a way through.

Some aspects of the Flexible Method will seem counterintuitive. When disaster strikes, we often instinctively revert to behaviour that might seem justified but which actually damages your organization in the long term.

We will unpack the threats of Covid-19, 9/11, Hurricane Katrina, the California wildfires, the Credit Crunch and Ukraine and offer real-world solutions on how to emerge stronger and fitter.

Despite the subject matter, this is a positive book that puts people at its centre – an approach I regard as crucial for success. By holding people at the very heart of your strategy and being more flexible in your thinking, I will show you how to make your organization more resilient.

I also reveal the secrets of strong, calm and purposeful leadership. Being humble and being prepared to listen and change is crucial.

Combined with this personal approach, leaders must apply ferocious determination – this is the essential counterbalance of the Flexible Method. It is the paradoxical blend of personal humility and kindness linked with radical determination which is precisely what gives this set of tools its power.

Real-life stories show how to communicate better with your team during a crisis, which will lead to a tighter, more trusting workforce in the long term.

I outline the best ways to protect your cash and keep your creditors onside, giving you room to move and be flexible as the situation evolves. I demonstrate how to set up strong business relationships to lean on as you steer through the crisis.

Examining lessons of past crises will show us how to think constructively about the future. A crisis is a time for deepening your core values, not abandoning them. The importance of maintaining your values during the crisis is a key factor for taking your team on the difficult journey with you.

In crises, winning organizations act like start-ups. I will show you how smart companies supercharge their creativity while supporting the mental health and wellbeing of their teams. We can turn disasters into opportunities. Handled wisely, crises can be a springboard for growth as you exploit once-in-a-lifetime opportunities offered in a post-crisis landscape.

Though painful, crises can actually be good for us. I don't say this lightly – like you, I carry my war wounds.

So let's take a journey through the darkest depths together and emerge fitter and stronger. I hope you enjoy the ride.

PART 1
The Gathering Storm

CHAPTER ONE

Prepare

It shouldn't have come as a shock.

In fact, Bill Gates gave a TED Talk on the next disease outbreak back in 2015 (Gates, 2015). He was standing in front of that now familiar ball of virus with those little suckers sprouting from it, saying, loud and clear, that we were not prepared for a pending global health crisis such as a pandemic.

If Covid caught you unprepared, you are not alone: national governments worldwide struggled to absorb the shock and failed to make plans or provisions. We were all caught out.

In her book *Preventable: How a pandemic changed the world & how to stop the next one* (2022), Devi Sridhar blames the catastrophic impact of Covid on a breakdown in global cooperation, groupthink among the scientific establishment and poor leadership skills of populist leaders.

Britain and the US were ranked the top two countries for pandemic preparedness but complacently failed to prepare for or respond to the unfolding situation in January 2020. Other countries like South Korea were more agile and quickly learned lessons from past SARS and MERS outbreaks.

Unfortunately, this pandemic will not be the last crisis we'll have to face. We live in an uncertain and increasingly unstable world and one thing is for sure: the next shock will come. In recent history we have lived through an oil crisis, a cost of living crisis, terrorist attacks, wars, natural disasters and the Credit Crunch. Now climate change is going to make hurricanes, fires and floods more frequent.

We face more wars, widespread economic and political instability, organized cybercrime and terrorism. We have seen how ransomware has become a real threat.

Perhaps the next crisis will come from disruptive technologies like artificial intelligence (AI). The brilliant Stephen Hawking warned of a wide range of future existential threats to humanity, including robots, genetically engineered viruses and asteroids.

As our planet becomes increasingly interconnected, with extended and vulnerable supply chains, an unexpected crisis has the potential to turn our world upside down without warning.

The first lesson to draw from recent events is that we must prepare.

In my company, as we have done after previous crises, we are using the Covid-19 pandemic as a vital lesson on how to plan for the next global crisis. Employing the Flexible Method, we chose to use the shock as an opportunity to change.

Preparing to defend yourself against a multitude of future threats can seem overwhelming, but doing nothing is not an option: preparation is the key to your organization's survival and long-term prosperity. You need to start this process well before the next storm hits.

In fact, you need to start it now. Your team will thank you for it when the next shock strikes.

Other companies were not as well prepared. The fitness industry, for example, was badly hit by the pandemic. John and Rob Grim are brothers who run Revolution, a chain of personal trainer studios in Sussex and London.

Rob: '*When I started to see the pictures come from Italy on Sky News it was suddenly apparent it was going to arrive on our shores.*

So it was like, goodness me, what's going to happen? And then sure enough, we started to have clients cancelling.

'*And then John and I were sat together watching Boris Johnson on 23 March 2020, the first lockdown, and we thought, what are we going to do with the business? I cried that day because the studios were going to have to shut. And I'm not someone who cries easily.*'

I can vouch for that. He is a tough, hard-working guy. As you will see, thankfully they later managed to adapt their business and pull through.

Disaster recovery plan

The first thing I encourage you to do to prepare is dust off or build your disaster recovery plan (DRP). I can hear you groan. We used to do the same whenever it was mentioned. It was one of those irritating things on our operations agenda, but in the pandemic we came to depend on it.

If your DRP helped you in the recent crisis, congratulations. If like many businesses you had to scramble and improvise to keep your business going, you may find some useful material here which will help you ask yourself a few key questions about your preparations.

And if you haven't got one at all, these DRP templates online will get you started:

▶ https://www.disasterrecoveryplantemplate.org/download/disaster-recovery-plan-template-basic/
▶ https://www.acutec.co.uk/wp-content/uploads/2019/06/Your-free-disaster-recovery-plan-template-1.pdf

As a responsible leader, doing nothing is not an option, so get your teams and your organizations crisis ready.

Argonon Group's DRP is a document on our intranet. We make it available to all newcomers in their induction.

It aims first to prevent or reduce the likelihood of a disaster by identifying threats and taking the necessary preventative actions, and secondly to ensure that Argonon and its associated companies are prepared to deal with an emergency effectively.

It will be used to support the recovery of Argonon following a major incident, defined as one which is outside normal operational and management controls and which is likely to compromise the operational capabilities of Argonon or require evacuation/partial evacuation of the premises.

Major incidents include:

▶ bomb threat
▶ power loss
▶ extreme weather, e.g. snow/ice/floods
▶ building fire
▶ infectious disease, e.g. Legionnaires' disease
▶ airplane crash.

The disaster planning team is made up of the Argonon board and the group senior management team across the various sites in the UK and US.

Your DRP should be as detailed as possible. And you must keep it updated. It should aim to include all eventualities.

Ask, what's the worst that can happen? Then develop a procedure for each scenario.

Think the unthinkable.

To make your plan as relevant and useful as possible it is best to expect the unexpected. There seems to be something inherently optimistic in the human brain that refuses to contemplate the likelihood of future disruptive events – despite overwhelming evidence to the contrary. Or maybe we just want to carry on with our day-to-day, ignoring these threats.

Brainstorm this with your team and then gameplay in real time. Dress rehearsing how your business would respond to these scenarios live will highlight what you are doing right. And crucially, what you have missed or are doing wrong.

Not everyone likes to admit faults, but I have learned to love mistakes and weaknesses. We all make them and we all have them. I see them as opportunities that we can turn into strengths. Mistakes and weaknesses are your friends – so bring them out into the open and use them.

Keep nimble. Restlessness is a gift. The pace of change has never been faster, so your DRP could be out of date sooner than you think.

Fresh eyes are always helpful for keeping you on your toes, so when new team members join the business, factor in a review. Your new employees may spot crucial gaps that have been overlooked.

Open this out across the business and ask all your departments to review the plan and add their thoughts to it.

Be transparent and open, involve the whole team. Being open and listening are key elements of the Flexible Method.

Make sure all employees are aware of the plan and encourage innovative thinking so they can react appropriately when every minute counts.

Invest in IT

When the next crisis hits, I believe that having the best IT systems you can afford will make your organization more resilient and keep your business up and running.

Communicating is the backbone of any business. You may need to work remotely for some months. Before the Covid-19 pandemic I imagine it would have been helpful to know how many of your team have good WiFi at home and to have upgraded it in advance where needed.

Microsoft Teams became our lifeline during the pandemic. We had migrated all our data into the cloud, so all of our post-production editing was able to flick to disaster recovery mode and our editors could work remotely by using Microsoft Remote Desktop through a secure VPN.

The scale of your organization will determine how much tech you need or can afford, but I recommend you listen to your IT-savvy advisors and friends and invest as much as you can.

Is your data secure? We store hours of research and filmed material and back it up every night to two separate locations in case of fire or a flood. I would strongly encourage you to store your data safely and not all in one place, so you have everything in duplicate.

We invest in cyber security software to shield the company from cyber-attack, phishing or hacks – a threat that I believe will only get worse in the future.

Safety net

As you prepare your business for future crises, create yourself a checklist:

▶ Do you have a succession plan for your leaders in case one or more of them is suddenly not able to work? Train staff to step in and step up. My global chief operating officer (COO) Laura Bessell, Finance Director Matt Richardson and I have agreed never to take a flight together again, for example.
▶ Is your insurance up to scratch?

▸ What will you do if all mobile phones go down?

▸ How would you communicate without the internet?

All this forward planning requires time and money, and to be honest it is not very nice to invite your team to a meeting to discuss death and catastrophe. But let's be pragmatic – this investment will help you adapt more quickly when the next crisis strikes. It will make your business more resilient – the key aim of the Flexible Method.

Remember that your customers won't hang around waiting while you recover – they'll go elsewhere. Conversely, seeing you have been smart enough to cope with the initial disaster will deepen their trust in you.

Your advance planning will be your safety net when the next crisis hits.

Flexible mindset

Flexibility is going to be the key to any success in times of emergency. Some of us have it in our DNA and have brought it to our business.

Ed Templeton has built a successful London restaurant business called Carousel. The concept is clever: the venue stays the same but each week a new chef comes to take over the kitchen and work with the team on creating their own unique menu for the week. It's a restless business model and has captured the imagination of many diners.

When the pandemic hit, Ed and his team, like everyone in hospitality, were badly hit. In fact, they were shut down completely and told they might not be able to open all year, which meant certain ruin.

Ed remembers: *'We had no disaster recovery plan to guide us. Everyone went into panic mode. None of us were prepared for anything of this scale.'*

But fortunately, they did have a flexible mindset and were well prepared psychologically and systemically for change. This proved to be a vital source of their recovery. If they had had a brittle mindset, they would have crumbled during the pandemic.

Another business leader with flexibility in her DNA is Fiona Allan, until recently chief executive of the Birmingham Hippodrome, a vibrant cultural hub in the UK. It puts on shows ranging from *Mamma Mia* to *Stomp!* and is also the home of the Birmingham Royal Ballet.

'The Hippodrome does have a disaster recovery plan and contingencies in place. We were well prepared for a bomb or a fire – we just needed to refer to page 330 to know exactly what to do – but a pandemic wasn't listed.

'OK, so Covid hit and the rug is just being pulled out from under you again, what do you do? I was able to call upon the fact that business as usual is not my usual. In fact, I think I personally thrive in change environments and I thrive on projects where I have scope to invent ways of doing.

'Of course, doing that under an actual global crisis pandemic was different, but I was able to call on my experience. Actually, I am a change leader and that is well within my comfort zone, so it didn't throw me.'

Not all managers are as flexible and their organizations are consequently more susceptible to shocks. If you recognize this as a weak point in your business, the good news is there are things you can do to make your organization more resilient to change and more flexible in its thinking.

Ensuring you do this is now a key part of being a leader, so it's time to move flexibility and crisis management to the front burner.

There are recognized methods for promoting flexible thinking for individuals, such as the Steel Man Technique. Its basic premise is that rather than start out by pointing out flaws in another person's argument, you first engage constructively with their case against you. Being sympathetic and exploring the strengths and weaknesses in their proposition, even bolstering their points of argument, enables you to better relate to their point of view. It builds rapport, increasing the chance of agreement, and tests our own assumptions and beliefs.

It's a more constructive approach than simply trying to win an argument.

For building flexibility into group thinking, try the Six Thinking Hats method developed by Edward de Bono, the inventor of lateral thinking (The de Bono Group, n.d.). Basically, it enables people to examine an issue from a variety of perspectives in a clear, conflict-free way, avoiding more brittle, reflexive positions.

You need to listen, be open and be willing to change yourself, of course. There's no point in listening to your team and then just carrying on regardless.

Heed the signs

Although disasters seem to strike out of the blue, with hindsight they are often predictable. Maybe it's that human optimism again, but we seem to have a tendency to think, it won't happen to me.

What I'm getting at is, counter the complacent mindset that tells you, it won't happen to me. Keep your eyes and ears open to world events. Watch out when there are emergencies in other countries. We heard about the Credit Crunch in the US long before we felt its effects in the UK. We are all interconnected as a planet now and we would be wise to stay alert to what is happening to others – because these things just may come our way too.

We were watching the news about Covid in January 2020. We were glued to the footage coming out of the hospitals in Italy in February. It was clear that this was a tsunami and was coming our way. Many governments failed to heed these signs and we lost valuable time as a result that could have saved lives. At Argonon we moved early – ten days in fact before we were forced into lockdown by government on 23 March 2020. These critical ten days made a huge difference to our outcome.

Among other things, we accelerated our shooting schedule. Ten days' footage in the can is a lot of material. When the networks were desperate for new shows, we were able to show them what we had and deliver it to them swiftly.

So, heed the signs and if your instinct says act, then start early. Your team will be reluctant to break from their busy routines, but take some time to prepare so you are ready to act decisively. And don't fall into the trap of 'planning for the last war' – stay flexible in what you do and how you do it. Being brittle will make your organization more fragile.

As you will already have experienced: when disaster strikes, you are going to need your systems in place, your team onside and every ounce of strength you can muster.

And you must act fast. The crisis will not wait for you.

Are you ready?

The Flexible Method tools – Prepare

▶ Move disaster planning to the front burner
▶ Brainstorm and rehearse possible scenarios
▶ Develop a flexible mindset
▶ Heed the signs
▶ See mistakes and weaknesses as opportunities you can turn into strengths

PART 2

Disaster strikes

CHAPTER TWO

Put your people first

On 11 September 2001, Michael Benfante was a 36-year-old branch manager at Network Plus when a jet smashed into his office building, the North Tower of the World Trade Center in New York (Ashlock, 2011).

Michael was on the 81st floor and the plane crashed just 12 floors above him. Everybody, including Michael, was petrified as raging noise and screaming filled the air. His first instinct was to send his people down. He shouted that they should all get out of the building, now!

He swept the room for his entire team, checking no one was forgotten, and hurried them into the hall towards the stairs. All 28 of them managed to scramble down the stairwell and out to safety. All 28 survived. But on the 68th floor, Michael spotted a woman who was not leaving. Tina Hansen used a wheelchair and could not evacuate without help.

He and one of his sales reps, John Cerqueira, then 22, strapped her into one of the light emergency wheelchairs that had been placed around the World Trade Center. They carried her down all 68 flights, one step at a time, surrounded by petrified crowds of people trying to escape. Their journey down took an hour and 15 minutes in increasingly dangerous conditions. They waded across

debris and sometimes water in the smoke- and dust-filled building, wending their way through offices to find new paths out.

After they delivered Tina safely to medical crews outside, there
was a deafening roar, suffocating clouds of dust and the two men
dived under a truck for safety just as the North Tower collapsed
over their heads and engulfed them. The truck saved their lives.
Tina Hansen also survived thanks to Michael's incredible selfless
heroism. I don't know about you, but I'm not sure how I would cope
under such unimaginable pressure. But Michael was quick-thinking
and had his heart in absolutely the right place. He knew he had to
get people to safety. I passionately believe that as leaders we must
ALWAYS put our people first.

At Argonon we have established a culture of putting people
first. This key element of the Flexible Method not only creates a
happier and healthier place to work, it has significantly contributed to our success. It is the very backbone of who we are and I
am convinced it can also make your organization more resilient.

Global fear

On 10 March 2020, as the Covid-19 pandemic was spreading
across the world, I vividly remember getting a phone call out of
the blue from Shirley Escott, COO of Leopard USA in New York,
one of nine production companies under the Argonon umbrella:
*'The team are frightened about coming into work on the subway
and on public transportation. They don't want to get into crowded
elevators. We are seriously thinking about making a radical decision and evacuating.'*

I could hardly believe my ears. But I listened carefully. *'We've
held a team meeting, everybody feels the same, we just do not feel
safe in the city.'*

Our offices were on the 21st floor of Grand Central Tower in midtown Manhattan. Our team of 200 staff would all commute daily from across the Tri-State Area. Many of them had been with the company for ten years or more. I know them personally and value each and every one of them. Their safety was paramount. *'We are planning to close down the offices immediately and send everyone home to work.'*

The scale of this decision came as a complete surprise. In London, we had already brought expert hygienic cleaners into our HQ to sterilize keyboards and door handles and we were planning a two-day dress rehearsal of sending our people home to trial working remotely. But evacuate completely?

Closing down the office might seriously impact our tight editing schedules that we were committed to. And when would the office ever reopen?

But if we ignored people's fears and told them they had to commute in, what effect would that have? I could imagine terrible family rows as a partner was forced to use crowded subways or buses. And if people were so worried, how could they concentrate on their work?

A big factor in our decision was that I trust Shirley. She is a seasoned professional and has a cool head. It didn't take me long to agree. And her foresight and the instincts of our New York team were spot on.

We decided to close all our offices, not just in New York but worldwide, and within 48 hours sent everyone home. This was two weeks before governments in the UK and the US launched their first lockdown.

Within two days of making this decision we had shifted our entire organization offsite and online, moving 1,500 logins to work from home, connected via Microsoft Teams by our IT department. Some people didn't have adequate WiFi signal or space in their home environment, especially those with children, so we gave them all advice, supplied them with equipment as best we could and sped up their connectivity, installing faster broadband in some instances.

Shirley says:

'It remains a source of pride that the New York office remained purposeful, professional and calm as we sent all staff home and the management team began the administrative and logistical operation of moving editing suites and laptops to home bases of editors and production staff.

'The reason it worked: teamwork, trust, cooperation and the fact that systems had been in place prior to Covid, which enabled us all to communicate with each other on a daily and sometimes hourly basis.'

It wasn't just about getting everyone up and running. It was an anxious time. People were scared, so as a next priority we gave everyone time to sort out their home lives – look after their families, make sure elderly relatives were okay, stock up on supplies, or make provisions for their children.

Shirley continues:

'Covid was an unknown situation. Government didn't know what to do. Information was coming at you from all sides and all places. And that's where one learned to take each day as it comes. As a TV producer, you plan, you think ahead, but you always have to pivot and react in the field because things change to a great degree.

'The most important thing I did was to get our staff home as soon as possible, to make sure they were safe. And then it was a matter of daily phone calls, daily communication, checking in.'

Shirley shows the Flexible Method in action here: preparation, putting people first, flexible thinking, calm, purposeful leadership and good communication all pursued with resolve.

When there is a shock, whether it's a terrorist attack, a war or another kind of crisis, your staff will be anxious and uncertain. They will look to you for reassurance. Putting their interests and safety first at this time of need is something they will appreciate and remember.

Enlightened leadership

Caring for your staff is not only the right thing to do, it is in your best interests. Being a strong leader who cares for your team leads to better staff retention and will ultimately give you a competitive advantage. If your staff are happy, they will not just be more productive, you will probably also have happier customers, which leads to higher profitability. So you could regard building a relationship with your employees as a good way of building one with your customers.

You can't fake a people-first culture. It isn't something you can just tell your HR department to implement using some miraculous new structure. Caring has to come from the top and filter down to create a culture of civility, cooperation and cheerfulness.

At Argonon, feedback and listening are crucial components of our culture. We not only get useful insights into how we are doing, our team feels included, valued and respected.

Having a good day-to-day rapport with your staff helps, so get out there and talk to your team. Be seen on the 'shopfloor'. Communicate with your people and let them know what is happening in the company and why. This streak of humility goes a long way and is a critical component of the Flexible Method leadership.

Many companies try to create a breakout space to encourage cooperation and collaboration, but in my experience the kitchen is the convivial heartbeat of the building. I try to head down there at least once a day to make a coffee or a soup and always end up chatting with people from every part of the group, from the receptionists, editors, producers to cleaners. You name it, we all muck in. It's always fun and I learn a lot from those chats. I know younger members of the team enjoy spending a little face-to-face time with me too. It's democratic and no frills.

Being an inaccessible leader is never a good idea and it can lead to terrible decision-making.

There are a lot of macho CEOs out there and I'm sure we've all worked for toxic bosses. I have had my fair share and know how debilitating and unproductive this can be. It is not what the boss does or says that will stick with you, it's how they make you feel – that is indelible.

Loyalty and respect are stronger binds than coercion and fear. Besides, does the world really need another tyrant?

Here are a few things you might consider for strengthening your workplace culture of caring and development:

- ▶ Build a better kitchen!
- ▶ Provide mentoring for junior staff and forge mutually respectful relationships with managers.
- ▶ Create wellness programmes to keep your people healthy and onside.
- ▶ Charity work in the community fosters team spirit and brings different hierarchies together, promoting interaction.
- ▶ Encourage some fun at work. Use humour.
- ▶ Team bonding will pay off in times of crisis or just day-to-day stress.
- ▶ Encourage open dialogue, critical feedback and innovation.

We spend a big chunk of our lives at work and a well-motivated workforce that wants to show up in the morning is vital, especially in a service industry. A happier staff will also be less stressed and therefore calmer in a crisis.

To perform at top level your team members need to think clearly and be free from any negative elements of stress. People get an enormous boost to feelings of wellbeing from performing at their best and being successful at what they do, so you can help create a positive spiral here.

All of this people-focused work will make your organization more resilient when the next shock strikes. Organizations full of stressed, demotivated staff will be more brittle and liable to crumble.

Eye of the storm

On 29 October 2012, Hurricane Sandy hit New York, flooding streets and subway lines, cutting power in and around the city and causing $65 billion worth of damage (Rice and Dastagir, 2013). Manhattan had a devastating power outage and everything below 32nd Street was plunged into darkness.

Our office was on 26th Street. We were out of power for several hours. All cell phones went dead. We tried calling our staff using the landlines that were still working. We didn't know where anyone was and were worried because contact was lost with our people. There was just no electricity in downtown Manhattan. We put our disaster recovery plan in place, then our COO at the time, Sara Banister, came up with a very effective, low-fi method of providing crucial information.

She stuck a notice on our front door on 26th Street. The notice said there wasn't anybody in the office and that we would post messages on Facebook and on the website as soon they could get power, and to check in every day, we're going to call you. In other words: don't panic, we're on it. We're going to fix things.

Simple. A few lines on paper glued to a door on the side-walk. I cannot tell you how many of our New Yorkers were relieved to see that little note. And then we called all the heads of departments and said, right, what can we do? And what can't we do?

The office was back after just four or five days. But it was a scary situation because people didn't know what was happening at first. Again, Sara put people first, demonstrated calm leadership, flexible thinking and good communications. Key elements of the Flexible Method.

We never had that breakdown in communication with the pandemic thanks to Teams. After Hurricane Sandy people headed to the office because that was the place where they sought help in the crisis. People just need someone to help them understand what to do.

Not only your staff but also your customers will notice and appreciate that you care about people. Especially when they are vulnerable and need help in a crisis.

Eruption

Access Travel Management is a bespoke travel agency based in Lichfield, Staffordshire, England. They specialize in corporate and media travel packages. They pride themselves on being 'insanely dedicated to our clients'.

In March 2010 the Icelandic volcano Eyjafjallajökull (love that name) erupted, sending an ash cloud miles into the sky. European airspace was closed as a safety precaution, stranding millions of passengers around the world.

Lee Gunn, Operations Director, Access Travel Management, remembers when he heard about the eruption:

'I was on annual leave when it hit. I did not instantly think, what does that mean for the business? Rather: what impact does that have for the people that we are going to have on the ground? What does that mean for our clients who we've worked with on getting those travel reservations and arrangements in place? What impact is that going to have on the rest of their schedule and the travellers themselves – are they going home to a family member? All of those different things start going through your head.

'For example, we had a doctor stuck in America where she was appearing as a contributor to a TV programme. She now desperately needed to get back to London for her day job. So obviously from the US to the UK, there's not many routes that you can go besides across the Atlantic. We were having to look at going through South America and across, but it was predominantly the UK inbound that was affected because of the ash cloud. We couldn't get anything for 48 hours and she was stuck there. But eventually because of the route that the cloud itself took we managed to route the passenger via Reykjavik back to London. So ironically going back through Iceland was the best solution.

'We had clients at MIPCOM, the big television festival in Cannes, France. People were hiring cars and driving up to Calais to take the ferry to the UK. Suddenly, there were no more cars available. There was a frantic panic and eventually we hired a coach and got them back that way.

'In these situations, where there is just kind of madness on the ground, it's critical to be able to take a step back from the situation and look at the bigger picture. For us, that was a map on the wall. How can we get people back to where they want to be using these ports, airports, using all types of travel, exploring all of the different avenues that we had available to us at that time.

'At our office it was all hands on deck, looking at who had we got where, who is going to be affected by this and who is it going to be an issue for? And then looking at what response do we need *for this? And we are extremely fortunate because of the ethos that we have across the organization to have a number of really passionate, dedicated members of the team. And without that, they'd become robotic, procedural and it wouldn't be a caring process.*

'Team members were offering to come in and help because they saw the news story and realized the impact for us as a business and our clients.'

So rather than a robotic response to the crisis, his company's culture enabled the travel agency to tap into a highly committed team willing to work really long and hard to help its clients. How was that fostered?

Said Said, Operations Manager at Access, outlines the company's approach:

'Every company needs to have the right team of people. When we recruit, we obviously need people who can book a flight, hire a car, etc. That's easy. They are the minimum requirements but not the fundamental. If you have no travel experience at all but you are ambitious and dedicated, I can teach you all of that stuff.

'I'd rather have a blank canvas with our new hires because we treat our employees like family. The way I run my team is I let them know exactly what we are facing. I let them know exactly how we are doing throughout the year. I tell them what kind of targets we've achieved. I make sure they are fed if they don't have time to take an hour's lunch break. We value them because it's them that make the company. Without them there is no company. We could have all the clients in the world, but if we have nobody to actually provide a good service, we have no company. Our people are our biggest assets.'

It is this focus on people that makes Access one of the leading media travel experts. In normal times, they deliver time and again. In a crisis, they know how to step up using key elements of the Flexible Method: putting people first, calm and purposeful leadership, flexible thinking, adaptability, and radical determination to implement their decisions.

It may be worth pausing here to ask yourself, do your people feel they are treated as your biggest assets?

Psychological impact

For teams to be resilient they have to feel it is worthwhile to make the effort to be so. They are more likely to do this if they are being valued and supported in a people-focused company culture.

A crisis places a lot of demands on staff to be adaptable, flexible and dedicated to their job. You must empower team members to take decisions. None of this is going to happen if managers view their team as automatons that have to be micro-managed.

During the Covid-19 pandemic, when teams were working remotely, there were stories of companies that intensified close supervision due to an inherent lack of trust, leading to greater job dissatisfaction and lower productivity.

If you need your team to think for themselves to solve problems and challenges, innovate and be creative, they need to operate with relative freedom.

Building team resilience depends on your leadership. Team members need to feel they are responsible for their collective future success and that everyone is looking out for each other in the process. Paradoxically, this means giving control, not taking it. In the process, you also have to establish clear mutual expectations about who is responsible for delivering what. During a crisis the message from you should be, 'We're all in this together!'

As a leader you must inspire, motivate, have the wellbeing of each team member as your foremost concern, and blend them together to become greater than the sum of their parts.

Especially when a team is working remotely, you will need to step up communication and display outstanding personal leadership. These are crucial subjects, so let's turn to them next.

The Flexible Method tools – Put your people first

▶ Establish a culture of putting people first
▶ Be seen on the shopfloor – humility is a critical leadership trait
▶ Feedback and listening are crucial
▶ Give control rather than micromanage
▶ Caring for your people is in your best interests

CHAPTER THREE

Lead with calm purpose

Even though we knew it was coming, we were still not prepared for the speed with which Covid ripped through our industry.

Overnight, my hectic world as CEO of a global media group shrank to sitting alone at home in front of my laptop. I felt very small.

With lockdown, all TV and film production shut down. Would it last forever? Was this how 20 years of toil was going to end?

How could we survive with no money coming in? I feared that my group might collapse. I wasn't even sure our society would survive, with the panic buying and some governments seemingly complacent and unequal to the magnitude of the task.

It was traumatic. It was heart-breaking. I felt completely powerless and disoriented.

My team and customers were just as scared and confused.

It could have been overwhelming. I had to muster up all my strength and step up.

No doubt you also had to dig deep during this time.

Calm leadership

Whatever you're feeling inside, in a crisis you must present a strong, calm and purposeful face to your team. Save the outpouring of your emotions for your most trusted inner circle or your loved ones. Channel your anxiety and fear into positive energy. Turn venom into rocket fuel!

At times like this people are crying out for clear, decisive and authentic leadership. But how are you supposed to respond to an all-consuming crisis?

First off: don't panic! Listen to your quiet inner voice. It's got you to where you are today. It will now help guide you in the darkest of times and help you navigate the road ahead. Do not look for quick fixes. This is crucial in these moments of crisis. I'm not suggesting you prevaricate either, as fast decisions may be required, but don't act in haste. Take the time you need to make a decision.

Take a deep breath, sleep on a major decision overnight if you can. Stress skews your brain. It's better to act at a measured pace on a good decision than rush into a bad one where the consequences could be unhelpful or even catastrophic.

The right mix

David Holt is mayor of Oklahoma City, one of the youngest mayors in America and the first Native American to hold this position. He is celebrated for his liberal-minded Republican stance.

He recalls: *'In the earliest days of the pandemic, people were scared of dying or having their loved ones die. It was a situation with heightened emotion and fear. The state government was really not stepping up into the breach. I'm the mayor of nearly 700,000 people who look to the mayor of Oklahoma City for leadership.'*

A difficult and delicate situation. '*It certainly called for every leadership and crisis management skill that I had. For me it was obviously very important to be communicative, to be talking to my residents.*'

Mayor Holt cites communicating frequently as a key factor of leadership and crisis management. '*Although I think you can communicate too frequently as well. It needs to be quality communications.*'

Mayor Holt is spot on here. You have to find the right balance of communication and not overly communicating or alarming teams where it is not necessary. Unless there was particularly urgent news, Mayor Holt would hold a weekly press conference with the head of the city health department as well as release daily social media posts.

'*I find that it's remarkable how many people were watching those press conferences and they felt calm about that. They felt assured knowing that their leader was on top of it, was engaged, was leading from the front.*

'*I would suggest a leader be literally up front, be on the front lines. Unfortunately, in March and April 2020 we all needed to be in our homes, so you couldn't necessarily be out there in the hospital corridors or anywhere else leading from the front physically, but you needed to be visible.*'

In a free, democratic country a mayor has to communicate important information, including, in this instance, persuading people to wear masks and stay at home. Mayor Holt says he spent a lot of time writing the scripts for his media and public appearances.

'*I thought it was important to be thoughtful about it, not just speak off the cuff. That's oftentimes how I communicate. I felt, in this context, I had to really think through what I was saying and how I was saying it. It was really important to show calm, "We've got this. We're in control of this", and to share knowledge and information.*

'And yet at the same time that you're showing strength and calm, you're also showing empathy. I remember speaking about what the next few days and weeks were going to look like and my voice cracked a little bit. I got a little emotional and it's funny, people still talk to me about that.

'For a certain segment of the population, probably not for everybody, they appreciated that very much. They don't want me to just sob on camera for 20 minutes. You got to find the right line. You got to show strength, but at the same time, you've got to show humanity, and finding that right mix is not easy. And it's not something you can really just teach someone. I think you have to come to it naturally or at least through experience.

'It is important for leaders to lead by example: that I follow my own precautions. You saw it across the United States. A mayor here, a governor there, they would have a weak moment, go to a party, or eat in a restaurant, not wear their mask at a certain critical moment and pictures would be taken, and suddenly they'd lost their credibility to lead. And it was really important to retain that credibility because it was saving lives. I was able to do that, and lead by example, and think what you were up against with the president at the time, and then state leaders here in Oklahoma. You were getting a totally different type of example at those levels.'

Mayor Holt's calm, purposeful leadership paid dividends. The death rate in Oklahoma City (1 in 448 people died of Covid-19) was below the national average (1 in 442) and even though it is the most densely populated part of the state, the rate was way below the Oklahoma state average (1 in 342) – a state where the governor chose very low engagement with the pandemic altogether. *'If the Oklahoma City metro had endured deaths at the same rate as the rest of Oklahoma, we would have lost at least 849 more residents in our city. 849.'*

Exemplary leadership indeed. I'm certain that his leadership throughout the pandemic, clearly validated by the relatively low death rate, demonstrates that humble, compassionate, robust leadership works. He put people first, showed calm and purposeful leadership, and followed through his decisions resolutely. The Flexible Method in action.

Lean on your experience

So where do you get these crisis leadership skills? As well as looking to exemplary leaders for inspiration, a good place to start is to look within.

The crisis may be unprecedented but many of us have built up valuable experience over careers of making considered, logical and (mostly) good decisions. We have survived the Credit Crunch, recessions, hurricanes, heatwaves, terrorist attacks, wars. The human race is remarkably resilient and so are you. Lean on your hard-won experience. It will stand you in good stead in a crisis and give you the confidence to lead your team through it.

When Covid hit, once we had moved all of our team offsite and online, I reached out to my senior management on Teams. It was important to touch base with them, check they were okay, their families safe.

I kept it very simple. I made sure I was dressed in my work gear, hair combed, beard looking smart. I even put on aftershave to make me feel good. A friend said to me, dress for where you are headed, not for where you come from. I took her at her word. I wanted to try to help things feel as safe as possible. I knew the team needed to see me calm and together.

It felt important not to overreact to the current situation. I tried to find a way to detach and think clearly about how we were going to navigate through the crisis. Talking calmly with the team and my loved ones was a great way to start to get perspective. The small details of these conversations were comforting and helped me to break the big picture into smaller, more manageable chunks.

What coping mechanisms have you found in your life? Were they helpful during the last crisis? How can you draw on them in the next one?

Lead with purpose

As well as demonstrating calmness, your leadership must have a purpose. This will make it credible. As you communicate you should make each step that you outline part of an evolving narrative towards targets and deadlines everybody can understand and buy into.

Our primary goal in the pandemic was to get our people back to work. But how could we achieve that?

I stated my genuine belief that I was confident that the organization would find a way through the crisis despite the uncertainty.

One step at a time

The truth is, we could not do everything at once. It was better to break things down into what needed to be done urgently, what could be done later in the day, what could wait until tomorrow and what could wait longer.

Start with the simplest tasks.

Fiona Allan, former CEO of Birmingham Hippodrome, vividly describes those first few days of the lockdown as she closed down her venue and cancelled dozens of shows:

'I think I was just dealing with each day as it came, I mean, this was such uncharted territory for us all. For the first week or two we were just dealing with the immediate intelligence that we were getting from government and the immediate things that needed to be done.

'In our case our biggest responsibility was to our own people and to make sure they were safe and at home, and we started having our first cases of Covid around about then. Of course, there were high levels of panic at that time and Covid was really hitting people very badly.

'We also had responsibility for the audiences and so our ticketing and sales team were engaged full time, moving and refunding tickets. As a sales staff they were very good at selling, but then suddenly their job became refunding people, which has less than zero job satisfaction. This was to last a year and a half and it was a very draining and horrible thing to have to be doing.'

At Argonon we also became expert at shutting things down but made it clear that this was a temporary measure. We wanted to give people hope. That felt very important.

If you shared this heartbreaking experience of having to close down parts of your business, how did you manage to keep up your team's morale? What lessons did you learn about leadership?

Set goals

Setting goals, even short-term at the outset, is critical. At the beginning of the pandemic, we set ourselves daily targets, including reaching out to everyone across the business, making sure everyone had access to Teams, speaking directly to every single client across the world.

Soon our goals became weekly. Translating government guidance into a company strategy, rescheduling filming on a production, identifying local crews in far-flung countries. And then, with momentum behind us and confidence building, those targets became monthly. I then set 1 June as a deadline for us to resume production.

We found that setting targets and deadlines that everybody could understand, buy into and collectively aim towards enabled us to move forward as a team in one direction. I believe this is the backbone of a calm, purposeful approach.

During a crisis, the best course of action is always to face up to the worst, be honest about the situation and don't try to hide from the dark stuff.

Empathize

This is very much a time for humility. Be human!

Remember first and foremost that there is a personal cost – not just a business one. Empathize with your people. Listen to their concerns. Some of our team were getting sick from Covid early on; one lost a loved one. We felt for them and shared it, discreetly. Nobody could be left behind in this tsunami.

Communicate clearly, frequently and frankly, while presenting a calm and purposeful plan of action.

I found an email to the team every morning was a good way to start. I wanted everybody in the group to know that I was there for them. A kindly, realistic voice in the silence, who was on their side, watching out for them and proactively seeking a way through.

Were you able to get an objective sense or concrete feedback on how you were perceived by your team during a crisis? It is hard to strike the right balance between empathy and strength. Communication is key and we will delve into it in detail later.

Stay credible

One course you should avoid is to simply pretend everything is going to be fine.

We all crave optimism, but there's no point in sugar-coating the situation. I made a point of rooting all my communication in the real world as things evolved. Anything less would have been dishonest and people need to trust and believe their leaders.

This doesn't mean you have to be a pessimist. Temper your optimism with realism – excessive confidence in such an obviously difficult situation would lose credibility.

Consistency counts for a lot. It is reassuring for your team and will help you steer a steady course.

Act with radical determination

Once you have identified those first steps, keep moving forward – don't look back, there's no time to waste. Your next actions must be carried out with kindness and empathy, but once the decisions are made, nothing must stop you pushing through the agenda to get the job done.

This is another of the pillars of the Flexible Method: fierce commitment to getting the job completed.

A crisis is always an opportunity to learn and try something different. Remember the firms that switched to producing PPE and sanitiser? We didn't do that in my organization, although we used plenty of both. But we did have a lot of original ideas and many of them came from my senior team, my generals.

I couldn't have done what came next without them.

The Flexible Method tools – Lead with calm purpose

- ▶ Present a strong, calm and purposeful face
- ▶ Don't rush into a bad decision under stress
- ▶ Face up to the worst but don't overreact
- ▶ Set goals
- ▶ Act with determination and get the job done

CHAPTER FOUR

Gather your generals

War cabinet

On day three of the first lockdown I was sitting in my spare bedroom at home in front of my computer, battling with an onslaught of challenges. The phone rang. It was one of my business partners at Argonon, Nick Godwin. He is creative director of BriteSpark Films, a documentary and current affairs producer. I was concerned by his serious tone: *'I had an idea. I wanted to run it past you. I was wondering if we should set up a "Cobra" team?'*

He wasn't referring to a snake; Cobra is an acronym for Cabinet Office Briefing Room A, used by the British government since the 1970s to deal with any major emergency. A kind of emergency war cabinet. *'There is a huge task ahead, James,'* he continued. *'I cannot imagine how much pressure you must be under. This might be helpful for you and good for the business.'*

I was interested in Nick's idea but needed time to think about it. The team would need to be very small to be effective and would need to contain a mixed group that was both highly skilled and fearless. We could frighten our staff by setting up such a team and thus admitting Argonon was now in a major emergency. Or perhaps people would think we were being over-dramatic.

I was also worried that if we invited just five or six executives to join this group, others might feel demotivated or alienated. Similarly, if I expanded the group, it would become diluted and lose its teeth.

It was a big decision and I spent several hours thinking it through. In the end I decided to proceed and invited my chief of operations, my most senior production executive and three business leaders from across the group, a mix of men and women. They covered the core areas ranging from operations to production, legal, financial and HR. Crucially, everybody in the team was bold and brave. There were no 'yes' people.

I invited them to a Teams call the following day. They all understood the concept of Cobra immediately.

It was a solemn moment when we first met. We talked of the lockdown, people getting sick, the collapse of production, and very quickly we moved on to what we were actually doing in real time to combat the crisis. It became immediately clear that each of the Cobra group had been preparing for the worst for several weeks. One of the team had vastly accelerated filming in February to get large stocks of quality shot material 'in the can', as we put it. That way editors could work from home, editing the footage through the spring and keeping the wheels turning.

This knowledge not only took some pressure off me, it bolstered our belief that we would do best if we responded flexibly to the crisis by taking small, incremental chunks of thought and action.

One of our Cobra group was my business partner Henry Scott, who runs the documentary company Like A Shot. He produces the hit series *Abandoned Engineering* in the UK and *Mysteries of the Abandoned* in the US. He can be ferocious in business so I am glad he is on my team and nobody else's. He said to me at that first meeting: *'James, we have to cut costs. All unnecessary expenditure must stop. Immediately. We will not survive unless we cut fast and cut hard. And the first cut is the deepest.'*

Painful but true. I knew this was coming and Henry was articulating the cold hard truth.

First up, I decided I would immediately cut my salary. You have to lead from the front. Then what?

We were going to do open-heart surgery on the entire business in a few short days, go meticulously through every single line of every single budget and take decisions. Cut? Or keep? Implications of both? This was an appalling prospect. I could feel the pain that was about to come. It was the right approach, I knew it. But it was a horrendous step to take. A horrendous series of steps.

When a crisis hits, gather your sharp brains around you and listen carefully. Be humble. Some of their ideas will be better than yours – that is why you hired them in the first place. At a time of crisis, you are going to need the hive mind of your top team.

You will most likely also need to listen carefully to those outside your business. Extreme pressure can bring out the best in some people, both inside your organization and in the wider community and online. People will be triggering exceptional ideas. Spread your net to capture the best information.

I have consciously built a team of A-list talent around me who have stacks of ideas and combine this with a willingness to challenge the norm and think disruptively. We also have built a deep-seated sense of mutual trust so we speak our minds freely. We don't always see things the same way. We have disagreements. But we talk them through and come up with the best solutions.

We met regularly in our Cobra group, our 'war cabinet'. The meetings were often an uncomfortable experience, to be honest. People said things I didn't want to hear and called on me to do things I didn't want to do. Like cutting salaries, laying off free-lancers, shutting down shoots. These impacted colleagues' lives and incomes.

Joey Attawia is strategic advisor for Argonon:

'Covid put us in a very difficult position because we were about to film major projects. It was a very scary time. The channels were very nervous because this was something that had never happened in our lifetime, so no one really understood it and therefore there was no real help out there. People were trying to figure out how we move forwards.'

Joey held detailed conversations with HR, legal and the producers across the group about how to continue filming while not putting people's lives at risk. Working closely with our head of legal, Amanda Goddard, we drew up a raft of measures to protect all our cast and crew during filming.

'It was all about talking it through and trying to understand what it was that we were trying to do, which was to stay afloat and keep people engaged because there was a real sense of panic. We had to steer a really steady ship.'

One of the shows was *Hard Cell*, a woman's prison comedy drama series starring Catherine Tate. This was a particular challenge as it was set in a women's jail where social distancing was going to be impossible.

'There was a lot of anxiety across the board. Drama is very, very much a hands-on industry. Hair and makeup, costume, props. And when you are dealing with artistic talent, we are not used to working in a vacuum. For us, everything is about being tactile. So people's thinking had to change. And if you are a talent, that sometimes can be very difficult because you are used to someone physically touching you, making you feel calm, making you feel important, making you feel everything's going to be all right, but that wasn't possible here.'

The show was eventually filmed with rigorous testing and hygiene measures in place.

'We needed a team in order to make the right decision because we needed to hear people's views. We needed to listen, whether we took their advice or not. But what it allowed us to do was to build a template, which everybody then used.'

Joey shows how we needed to look at all options to find the right one and that people were fearful and needed to be taken on a journey when many people in our industry were giving up filming and shutting down.

When applying the Flexible Method, flexible thinking requires calm and purposeful leadership, a people-first, 360-degree approach to the challenge at hand. Then you need fierce determination to execute the method with 100 per cent conviction.

It is not easy, but it works.

You may already have emergency response teams in place – especially for IT outages – and if you have prepared well for a range of disasters, you will have procedures and checklists which emergency response teams have practised.

Most large organizations create crisis management/emergency response teams to identify a wide range of situations that could affect the organization and then come up with a comprehensive plan for dealing with these events – for example, fire, industrial accidents, natural disasters or supply chain disruptions.

The 'generals' concept is a higher-level group specifically gathered for the crisis at hand.

Have you thought about who would be in your Cobra team? They must be outspoken thinkers who are not afraid to tell you the worst – and then come up with solutions. Toxic doom merchants or naysayers should not be invited. What you want are fearless, confident and constructive people of action. People who, once the decision has been made, will push it through relentlessly.

I would be stringent in your selection. You only have room for five or six. The Cobra group members should:

▶ understand the big picture
▶ have in-depth knowledge of their area of responsibility
▶ be good collaborators
▶ be strong communicators
▶ handle pressure well
▶ think fast and analytically.

Select your group to fit the specific situation. Some crises could be more IT or PR focused, for example. Typical areas of responsibility represented could include:

▶ HR
▶ legal – to check the group's actions do not put the company on the wrong side of the law
▶ IT – crucial for remote working
▶ finance – for keeping you afloat
▶ an internal and external communications expert.

You are going to have to really trust your group and be a good listener when they put forward their ideas. Part of creativity is developing original answers to difficult questions. Flexible thinking is everything.

And just because someone isn't from a 'creative' area doesn't mean they can't think outside the box and solve problems. HR and finance may be very process-oriented but they can also help you transform your business using lateral thinking.

Emotional traps

Just as stress is not conducive to clear thinking, we must also be aware of emotions clouding our judgement. Emotions are heightened during a crisis and they have a powerful effect on how we think.

Can you recall a time when you felt emotional and noticed that you were twisting facts to support what you wanted to hear? When you wanted something to be true despite all the evidence?

Psychologists call this motivated reasoning and ironically, people with expertise can be rather good at it because we can marshal more reasons to believe whatever we really want. This is manipulative and unhelpful.

I'm not suggesting you become an emotionless computer; just be aware of how you are feeling when faced with information. Is it making you feel angry, scared, elated? Then understand that these feelings can skew your judgement.

AVOID GROUPTHINK

This is where your generals can really help. To avoid groupthink, you need to choose radical, bold minds for your war cabinet, not just people who make you feel comfortable.

FACTORS THAT FAVOUR FOCUS

There are a number of factors that will help your war cabinet come up with innovative solutions. To paraphrase Samuel Johnson, a crisis certainly concentrates the mind.

Your group should share:

- ▶ a clarity of purpose to focus on what really counts, right here, right now
- ▶ a sense of urgency, cutting out distractions and non-essential verbiage
- ▶ a drive for simple, robust solutions that can be rolled out quickly
- ▶ a commitment to repurpose existing technologies or structures rather than invent things from scratch. Maximize what you have available to you.

Crises tend to break down silo mentalities and promote levels of open-minded collaboration that are difficult to achieve in normal times (do you remember 'normal times'?) You should have zero tolerance for turf wars or defensive departmentalism.

Because of the inherent uncertainty created by a crisis there is less fear of failure. You will have no choice but to embrace the uncertainty. It may well lead to rapid learning and better outcomes.

THE POWER OF DIVERSITY

A diverse team will give you the competitive edge. You need a full range of ideas and experience, especially in a crisis.

I believe passionately in the value of diversity and we have built it into our annual 'Argonon for Everyone' campaign to boost diversity in our group. We have a strong track record on diversity and inclusion across our business. We have many senior women leaders, a large number of people from lower social-economic backgrounds, a mixed workforce including people of colour, many different races and religions, we represent LGBTQI+ well, and disability is a priority for us, with more work to be done.

Your diverse team will ensure you have access to the broadest range of ideas and skills. This will increase your ability to problem solve and avoid groupthink.

You cannot afford anything less.

INCLUDE ALL YOUR GENERALS

The Cobra team is deliberately designed to be small and intensely focused, but it would be a mistake to exclude your other skilful generals. So for them, I set up a weekly Teams meeting with 40 of my senior leaders.

The agenda of each meeting was to run through what each business unit was doing – even the smallest detail would provide evidence that we were moving forwards. As each unit provided one nugget and then another, before long we had a list of small things, which as a whole felt like progress. It was evidence of positive progress and definitely gave us all hope. Celebrating small wins is good for morale.

As the weeks went by, the list of nuggets got longer until we could feel a real sense of forward momentum.

Unexpected dividends

When you empower your generals, you will be stronger. They will help you be your best self. They will in turn help your company be its best self and operate at peak performance. This must be your positioning in any emergency situation.

Here are some ideas that stemmed from our group coming together and brainstorming what looked like insoluble problems at the time.

Although all filming was locked down in March 2022, there was one exception to the rule: news and current affairs crews could get special dispensation passes allowing them to move freely around cities, including filming in the street. This was seen as an essential public service.

So overnight Nick Godwin and his team at the production company BriteSpark pivoted. They transformed themselves into a current affairs outfit that would serve a vital public service.

They went on to produce films such as *What Is It Like to Catch Coronavirus?* which investigated the symptoms of Covid-19 (when there was still an appalling lack of information available). Six families and individuals from different backgrounds filmed themselves battling the virus. Scientists and experts helped explain their symptoms and how the disease progresses, and why some people are affected so much more seriously than others.

They also made *Coronavirus: How Britain Is Changing* for the Channel 4 documentary series *Dispatches*, investigating what a post-Covid-19 Britain, torn apart by the disease, might look like, from seismic changes in economic policy to shifts in the way we view and treat other people, and the widening of the gaps between rich and poor.

There was so much disinformation around and poor communication from government that BriteSpark could cut through the noise and provide us all with much-needed and trustworthy journalism.

They did such a useful job that Channel 4 commissioned many current affairs films from BriteSpark (and still does) and Nick and his team found a way to keep bringing in the money, despite the lockdown.

HOUSE HUNTERS INTERNATIONAL

Our successful US show *House Hunters International*, produced by Leopard USA, set up a global tracker of lockdowns as they came into force in every country around the world – crucially monitoring lockdowns daily and spotting when they were lifted, making it possible to film again. Some countries would be going into lockdown just as others were lifting restrictions. The production team updated the list constantly and shared it with the whole group. It was fascinating to see South Korea open up, Sweden stay open, New Zealand open and then close. A fluid and constantly fluctuating picture. Talk about flexible thinking needed!

The production team pivoted, researched films that could be produced in Taiwan, or Guatemala, stocked up on Swedish stories, shelved Germany, France and Italy for a future date and so on. Their filming schedule became a flexible piece of elastic, with things moving in and out at high speed. It meant the show was able to continue filming somewhere on the planet throughout the Covid pandemic, using local crews rather than flying teams in.

WORZEL GUMMIDGE

We were able to film the scripted series *Worzel Gummidge* on location by introducing stringent hygiene protocols on closed sets, despite the BBC warning there would be no drama series shot in 2020 as it was just too risky. It was the first original drama series out of the gates.

The Covid protocols we developed helped reassure the BBC and eventually they gave us permission to film. These protocols were first suggested by the Cobra team. No one got sick during the shoot – helped by the outdoor summer locations. We produced the show successfully and received a spectacular response from the audience.

THE MASKED SINGER

Resuming filming for *The Masked Singer* during the pandemic presented a whole different raft of challenges. We had to significantly beef up our Covid protocols to shoot it inside a studio with lots of makeup and costume staff. The protocols worked. Once again no one got sick. Once again the ideas originated from the Cobra team.

ATTENBOROUGH AND THE MAMMOTH GRAVEYARD

We filmed a documentary for BBC One and US network PBS called *Attenborough and the Mammoth Graveyard* with British national treasure and environmentalist David Attenborough – despite the fact that he was 95, shielding and uninsurable due to the insurance industry dropping all their support for production. We transformed his garden shed into a connected, fully interactive sound booth, which he absolutely adores. He can continue work now, whatever the world throws at him, and starts another new chapter in his illustrious career.

Hidden generals

If you manage a small team, you may not have a group of generals to lean on. If you have a smaller organization, you could also look outside to see if there are any potential generals you can call on to help.

Have you thought about who you might call up to help you in the event of an emergency? These might be kindly people outside your organization who have specific skills that could help you, or indeed save you. It is worth thinking this through.

In August 2005, Hurricane Katrina hit the US Gulf Coast and flooded New Orleans, causing more than $100 billion in property damage and killing more than 1,800 people. Around 80 per cent of the city's population was forced to evacuate (Wikipedia, nd).

Pastor Alex Bellow and his family were caught in the middle of the devastation: *'Katrina made everybody equal. We all were in a destitute place. We all lost everything.'*

The federal government bungled its response, leaving people in a desperate plight. The Federal Emergency Management Agency (FEMA) was led by officials who were political appointees with no experience of disaster management. Confusion among different levels of government paralyzed decision-making and efforts got tangled up in red tape. About $2 billion spent by FEMA after Hurricane Katrina was wasted or fraudulently claimed, according to *The New York Times.*

So where was the leadership? And where were the generals? Fortunately, the true generals were there, only hidden. It needed someone with foresight to identify them and call them up for service.

With infrastructure badly damaged and the government response ineffective, the NGO World Vision came up with a bold solution. It would find and enroll leaders on the ground, namely 100 pastors, the hidden generals, among them Alex Bellow. Rooted in their community, willing, trusted and able, they would become the responsible experts on the ground who could rally volunteers, medics, teachers and families and provide a framework to roll out the package of rescue measures.

Even though churches throughout the disaster zone were badly damaged, they and their pastors still functioned as community hubs, a great place for communication, support, intelligence and sharing resources.

World Vision decided to focus their rescue efforts on the pastors and their churches, right at the heart of where emergency relief was needed urgently. Who would have thought of turning a community of pastors into a network of generals?

Alex remembers:

'It was ground zero. I was one of their first pastors. I just started getting inundated with needs. And somehow World Vision found me and said, "Pastor, we need to get supplies into the community. Can we send it to your church? And can you get it out?" And I said yes.

'And then they came back and said, "Okay, our donors have raised $3.2 million and so we are dividing that between Louisiana and Mississippi. It's going to be $1.6 million for Louisiana, and $1.6 million for Mississippi." And they asked me to oversee the distribution of the $1.6 million for Louisiana in the form of $50,000 grants to churches.'

Empowering the pastor-generals became the backbone of the rescue mission.

Alex continues:

'I always had the philosophy that if I'm going to call myself a leader, I got to be able to roll up my sleeves and just get my hands dirty and work. And I think my reputation may have preceded me. And once they started sending trucks, I was the first person that hopped on and started cutting the shrink wrap and getting the pallet jack and moving supplies off and into the hands of the people who needed it.

'In the initial aftermath of the storm it was what we call cleanup kits. That's for people who did have something to return to, like

their house wasn't completely destroyed, where they definitely had a cleanup job ahead of them. So, World Vision created clean-up kits, and that's basically all of the supplies that you need to do a thorough cleaning after a massive flood event came into your home. Also some non-perishable food plus clothes, shoes, socks, hygiene items, just the real basic stuff.

'As we progressed further into the recovery and people started rebuilding their houses, insurance started showing up and they started getting funds to rebuild. Then we provided building supplies to put a house back together. And then the next stage was giving them furniture. All brand-new stuff from our generous donors who saw the massive needs in our community and rose up to meet those needs.'

This effort is a powerful example of putting people first and flexible thinking backed up by a robust method of distribution. The Flexible Method in action.

In total, World Vision distributed $9 million in goods to 318,000 survivors in the Gulf region plus $1.5 million in grants to help churches and families get back on their feet, headed up and managed locally by the pastor-generals and their teams. The effort was gargantuan, pursued with urgent determination and tirelessly enacted.

What these guys achieved dwarfs our modest efforts at Argonon in pivoting our programme-making during the pandemic, but we share some key elements of the Flexible Method: they thought the unthinkable, used innovative brainstorming to find a way through a crisis, identified and deployed a coordinated team of generals to implement, and turned the disaster around. They far outperformed the might of the US government's relief efforts. It really is inspiring.

Creativity usually comes about through collaboration. I'm sure you can recall instances of a conversation unexpectedly leading to a surprising solution. When a crisis hits, you want to supercharge this process with your handpicked team, even if you have to reach out and find them externally. Help is out there when you give yourself the space to think carefully.

Once you have solutions, the next step is to empower your team to execute, delegating and spreading the decisions across the entire organization.

In the next stage of this process, excellent communication will be the way to cascade the Flexible Method through your management structure to make sure everybody is informed and on board.

You are going to need all of your team on side for the next stage of this journey.

The Flexible Method Tools – Gather your generals

▶ Gather your top team at your side
▶ Empower your bravest thinkers
▶ Listen humbly and carefully and be open to radical ideas
▶ Avoid 'yes' men and doom-mongers
▶ Avoid groupthink
▶ Delegate and act decisively

CHAPTER FIVE

Communicate, communicate, communicate

Producer Shirley Escott was woken by a violent jolt. She sat up in her hotel bed as the room shook, radiators rattled and a large pitcher of water crashed to the floor from her nightstand. A 7.8-magnitude earthquake had just struck the South Island of New Zealand.

Recalling that night in 2016, Shirley, COO of Leopard USA, says:

'It was terrifying. The first thought is call everyone. Is everybody okay? But how was I going to communicate with everyone? We were in different hotels. I wasn't sure who was actually on location because art department, hair and makeup, wardrobe, would have been there earlier than anybody else. So that was a very scary time.'

The crew were spread over a 20-mile radius of the set, filming the mini-series docudrama *The Men Who Built America: Frontiersmen.* Shirley jumped on the phone, checked there were no injuries, or worse, and then called an emergency meeting. Her first decision was to close down the shoot. Mudslides had made many roads impassable and production was unthinkable.

'I learned it's about making decisions quickly in the field and holding to those decisions, being clear what those decisions are and

communicating that. Make sure your key people are in touch with their teams and inform you immediately if there's any concern.'

This was communication at its most basic and urgent level.

I've already said a lot about communication as it plays a big role for leaders at all stages of a crisis, and it is such a crucial element of the Flexible Method that I'd like us to focus more on it here.

A voice in the dark

I'm sure you can vividly remember the raw fear that pervaded when the pandemic took a grip in March 2020. People were scared to come into the office or use public transport. There was panic buying in supermarkets, and we had no idea what the death toll was going to be or if we would ever get a vaccine.

At Argonon we were concerned about people struggling to work at home with their children off school during lockdown. Everybody was anxious about losing their jobs. We assured our full-time staff that they would continue working or be furloughed if possible. HR worked every day to communicate with staff on an individual level.

For parents juggling work with children at home, we gave them a lot of support and flexibility during the pandemic to ensure their requirements were met. We also had people with family in hospital or on ventilators that needed support. It was a stressful time, as I'm sure you remember only too well.

During a crisis, people have a heightened need for good, honest communication that gives them information, guidance, helps them adjust and cope emotionally. It puts their experience into context and helps make it more manageable.

As a leader, that's a huge weight of expectation on your shoulders. I'm sure you felt the burden of it too. The pandemic put executives under intense public scrutiny as companies were judged for the care, authenticity and sense of purpose they demonstrated.

Crises can produce great leaders and communicators whose words and actions give comfort, restore faith and are long remembered. Ukraine president Volodymyr Zelensky is a recent inspiration. Contrast him with Vladimir Putin, who is stiff, remote, emotionless, an insular, top-down leader who opposes transparency.

Zelensky comes across as a humble, humane family man who communicates authentically. We see him leading from the front and appealing emotionally to the world. His message is one of collaboration, shared goals and teambuilding. A master class in crisis communications.

We can't all be Churchillian, but in a crisis you are going to have to significantly step up communication with your stakeholders.

A note of caution before you channel your inner Zelensky: just pause and be clear about your strategy before pressing 'send' amid all the uncertainty and anxiety of the situation. Your communications need to be effective and appropriate for the moment. When the team get a note from you, every word matters.

The content of your communications will change as the crisis evolves. I have found it is best to tailor communications to each situation and each group of people I am addressing, bearing in mind their likely emotional state at the time. Focus on what they need to know at that specific moment in time.

Early-stage crisis communications

I know that I felt very alone at the start of the pandemic in March 2020. My partner and I were locked down in our house outside of the city. All my team were locked down in theirs. I made sure my mum had got to a safe place with her partner in the countryside and that my closest family and friends were okay. We all did a lot of ringing around at that time.

I felt acutely concerned about the more junior members of our team. TV is a young industry and a lot of our staff are under 30. I knew they must be frightened and feel isolated. So I decided to start writing a morning email to my entire team, across the globe. I would speak frankly and openly. And so began a series of letter writing that continues today. It is a very personal, lo-tech way of connecting with everyone on the team.

I found it therapeutic to be honest and got a lot of positive feedback, often from junior members of the team, who appreciated that the boss was reaching out to talk with them. I was truly present for them.

This was one of the first:

Email to Argonon staff on 24 March 2020, 11:49

We urge you to follow the guidelines, keep safe and respect social distance.

Argonon is moving forwards and we are trying to keep as much business running as possible. It is important we stick to delivering our shows which means keeping edits on track and thinking laterally when we have to work with the footage we have got. Across the board, we are encountering difficulties filming and this will likely go on for some months.

Separately to that we are looking at ways to mitigate downturn in revenues by working up our back catalogues and reversioning and updating archive shows. There is an appetite

---

for this at the networks who themselves face challenges with pipeline.

We are having to make some tough decisions and we are doing all we can to mitigate them. Thank you for your ongoing teamwork.

Please keep in close contact with your line managers and keep positive. We will get through this.

With best wishes,

James

James Burstall, CEO, Argonon

Your communications should focus on giving people necessary information while encouraging them to remain calm and stay safe. Your stakeholders will have limited attention in a breaking crisis as there is a lot is going on and they may feel frightened and overwhelmed. They are not going to be in a state to process complicated information, so keep messages simple, to the point and actionable.

In a crisis you are going to need to communicate with your staff much more often than you probably think is necessary. Frequent communication reduces fear and uncertainty and ensures that employees have heard the message.

If your communications are going to be effective, your audience must trust you and what you are saying, especially in a crisis. Be honest about where things stand, don't be afraid to show vulnerability, and maintain transparency.

You must give credible and relevant information. If people believe you are misleading them or downplaying risks, they will lose trust. Don't sugar-coat the situation with false optimism. If things are unknown, don't speculate. Acknowledge bad news and uncertainty.

Email to Argonon staff on 27 March 2020, 09:18

Today I want to thank our Operations Teams across the UK and the USA for their meticulous, considerate planning and deep thinking. From COOs to MDs, Heads of Production, Production Managers, Ops Manager, Facilities Manager, Line Producers, Coordinators, Assistants and others, your patience and bravery are monumental. You have been faced with so many challenges recently and you stand strong.

We produce the series *Monster Moves* with Windfall – who would have imagined events would come upon us and force us to perform our very own Monster Move – pivoting Argonon, this highly geared, complex, sensitive and deeply rooted eco-system from one place to a completely new one? And yet, here we are, under way with this very thing.

Today is going to be another difficult day, I cannot deny that. We are still facing pretty much total shutdown of filming for April, May and June, which means we cannot, for now, film and deliver our shows and that means we do not get paid. We hope we will be starting to film again in July, although that is not certain. Livvy in New York and Jo in London are starting to put together a Filming Permit Daily Update, as we are getting intel that some territories around the world may release filming permits, in a limited way, for local crews in the coming weeks. We are going to monitor this closely and will share intel around the group as it becomes available.

In the short term, though, we are needing to make painful changes. We are doing everything we can to mitigate this and our trusted Operations Teams and your line managers will keep you closely informed. The UK and US governments have announced some helpful measures of support and we will navigate these with you.

I wanted to share one thought with you. I was having a tricky time at Banff TV Festival in Canada a few years ago and I called my sister Sarah in New York. She is the most widely read person I know, living many years in America now, a naturalized American citizen. She listened carefully, was kind across the thousands of miles, and she then gifted me the words of Mary Wollstonecraft, an 18th-century English writer and thinker (and mother of Mary Shelley who wrote *Frankenstein*). Mary Wollstonecraft is widely regarded as the founding feminist philosopher and she wrote:

'The beginning is always today.'

Powerful words.

I share them with you in the hope they will be helpful as we start yet another new chapter today. And remember, all that is happening in the world is temporary and will pass. We must cherish each other and give thanks. Things are changing and yet we are all at the beginning, together.

James

One way of offsetting bad news is to remind people of times when they overcame challenges in the past, during previous crises, for example.

People tend to pay more attention to positively framed information, so tell people what they should do rather than what they *shouldn't* ('do's' rather than 'don'ts'). For example, the US state of Oregon's Covid slogan, 'Don't accidentally kill someone', was criticized for using unnecessary negatives.

Repeat and reinforce messages. You may get tired of repeating your key messages, but your stakeholders need to hear them several times.

People will be looking to you for guidance and support. *What* you say and *how* you convey it will play a significant part in determining how your organization performs during these difficult times.

Show empathy. Acknowledge fear, pain and suffering. State up front what your organization's objective is in this emergency and commit to achieving it.

Don't spill your guts!

Demonstrating vulnerability, sharing your feelings and acknowledging emotional turmoil can help build trust, but you need to be careful not to go overboard here.

A textbook example of the dangers of doing this came from Tony Hayward, CEO of oil giant BP, with his remarks after the Deepwater Horizon oil spill in 2010. Following the worst spill in US history in the Gulf of Mexico, he gave an almost textbook demonstration of how *not* to conduct public relations.

After appearing to try to duck responsibility for the disaster, he tried to downplay the scale of the environmental damage by stating correctly but insensitively that the ocean was a very big place. He then topped it off by complaining that he wanted to 'get his life back' (Kanter, 2010).

Transparency

Share different strategy options you are considering when faced with the crisis. Transparency builds trust and shows respect for employees by assuming they are sufficiently intelligent and resilient to cope with this openness.

People will be worried about their jobs. Reassure team members that their employment is secure if this is the case, otherwise tell them straight as soon as possible so they can plan accordingly.

At Argonon these very difficult, sensitive, painful conversations were done directly through the independent production companies within the group. Jenny King, head of HR at Argonon clarifies:

'These companies have their own identity, and the majority of the freelancers have direct relationships with the heads of production, line producers, heads of development, etc. So we approached it from the perspective of supporting those people within the business who were having to have those difficult conversations because it made it personal.

'We avoided a blanket approach. It wasn't an anonymous email coming from the HR department or senior management to say, "Unfortunately we're shutting down the production because of the pandemic and we no longer need your services".

'It was a personal approach that was taken, and I like to think that people appreciated that, because so often you run the risk of it becoming faceless by sending out mass communications from a management team or from an HR team. What's always been really important to Argonon as a group is our people. They're our biggest commodity and they're what makes us what we are. So you need to look after them.

'I was regularly checking in with the heads of production to make sure that they had the support and the tools that they needed to have these very difficult, sensitive, painful conversations.

'I had a good understanding of the legislation as well. So I had the technicalities of it sorted and it allowed them to speak to somebody who was involved but slightly removed at the same time, because sometimes those conversations need the emotion taken

out of it so that people can make sense of it. I would send out updates on changes to legislation because wading through this is a headache. It's very, very technical and people just wanted an easy answer.

'I would also send out regular communications to people literally saying, "How are you?" It went out to everybody and I got good feedback from that. It made people feel connected. And nothing was knee jerk; everything was very, very clearly and calmly thought through.'

Through these difficult times Jenny followed the Flexible Method, putting people first and communicating calmly and transparently. She was a great resource for Argonon during the pandemic.

Mid-stage crisis communications

As the crisis evolves, leaders should help people cope emotionally with the trauma of sudden change and adjustment to the 'new normal'.

Allow employees to be able to express their concerns to leaders without fear of damaging their careers. Feedback channels can include your HR department, a regular one-on-one meeting with a manager, or an anonymous suggestion channel.

Soon after the first lockdown kicked in, we set up a whole range of meetings for people to attend. There was the 40-strong senior leadership team meeting, online of course, where all the heads of department could share some of the latest intel.

Then I set up a number of weekly one-to-ones with my head of HR and head of legal and commercial. I wanted them to feel supported as well as sharing important operations news. Our global COO Laura and I talked every day.

When restrictions were lifted briefly in the spring of 2020 and we were allowed to meet one person outside, she and I bought take-away cocktails and tramped round the streets of central London. It was a lot of fun – and we got the job done. A Negroni has never tasted so good in a plastic cup and drizzly rain.

Periodically reporting back with feedback and follow-up actions will build trust in your leadership – not only during this critical period but also continuing after the crisis.

As the crisis deepens you will need to build resilience in your team, foster a sense of hope and optimism to supercharge creativity, and plan for the future.

Celebrate the positives, even small wins. Share uplifting moments about how your people are adapting to new ways of working.

Email to Argonon staff on 30 March 2020, 10:50

I hope you had decent weekends and managed some rest.

After a very difficult week last week, we managed to pull out of the hat some remarkable creativity in two Argonon premieres on Sunday.

[I then highlighted *The Snow Spider* from Leopard Pictures, a beautifully crafted magical scripted series for the BBC set in rural Wales, and Windfall Films' new series *Secrets of Egypt's Valley of the Kings* which aired on Channel 4.]

Now we get down to the nitty gritty of daily life under lockdown. I hope you will manage this time well. Getting the balance right between focused work, regular exercise and some time out is going to be important. We are in this for the long haul.

Today, I want to thank our Finance, HR, Legal and Business Affairs teams. Many of you have been working flat out through the last weeks and again this weekend to get us to a place where we are safe and protected. Our income has dropped significantly and will do for the next three months as events beyond our control enforce a temporary hiatus on filming.

Now more than ever we need to know we can rely on our management accounts to keep us all informed, paid, protected.

In return, I ask everyone please to continue to do everything possible to deliver shows, keep costs down to a minimum and to see what we can conjure up in development to engage our buyers with fresh ideas. I am already hearing about some of these ideas – and having some myself. There is nothing like duress to trigger creativity.

We need to seize this moment and give it everything we've got.

I hope you will be proud of our two premieres this weekend. You are all part of the team that produced them. And remember: the beginning is always today.

James

As well as publicly thanking staff, speak to them directly or send personal thank-you notes.

Action reduces anxiety and can restore a sense of control, so give people relevant, constructive things to do. This could involve helping others affected by the crisis.

Encourage a sense of common social identity and belonging based on shared values of mutual support and achievement.

End-stage crisis communications

As people adapt, focus increasingly on helping them to make sense of their experiences in the crisis. Highlight the shared sense of purpose, how your organization has responded, and set out your plan for the future with two or three simple goals.

Set out a clear vision for how your organization and its people will emerge.

You must then take actions to realize those goals because communication consists not only of words but also actions and people will take note of what you do to follow up on your words. Anxious about the organization's future, they will look to you for hope, so convey a compelling message and connect to a deeper sense of purpose.

And once again, be sure to praise colleagues who have shown particular dedication or achieved outstanding results.

How did you communicate during Covid? Is there anything you learned that you will use in your communications during the next crisis?

Communications may well be your most important skill as a leader. Following the Flexible Method will help guide you as you communicate by putting people first, showing calm and purposeful leadership, and then following through on your decisions with resolute commitment.

But no matter how eloquent or empathetic you are, words alone will not keep your business running in a crisis. For that you will need hard cash – a subject we turn to now.

The Flexible Method tools – Communicate, communicate, communicate

▶ Work out your comms strategy and then act on it
▶ Change your communications as the crisis evolves
▶ Empathize
▶ Demonstrate vulnerability and transparency
▶ Set up regular one-to-ones with your core players
▶ Set out a clear vision for the future

CHAPTER SIX

Protect your cash

Lifeblood

I've tried to leaven the bread in this book with a little behind-the-scenes showbiz glitter, but in this chapter it's time to get out the ledgers, roll up our sleeves and get down to the nitty gritty. Behind every business there is a P&L (profit and loss).

Cash flow may not be sexy, but where would creatives be without it? If creativity is the heart of a business, money is its sinews, or lifeblood.

Even the hip-hop group Wu-Tang Clan understood this with their hit *C.R.E.A.M. (Cash Rules Everything Around Me)*. I wouldn't quite go that far, but as a businessman money is important to me. I respect it and treat it carefully. I am not in love with money. For me it's a vehicle to do good things – to be generous, to be creative, to nurture, support, build. It is a means to an end.

Money gives you freedom to make better choices.

But in a crisis, money – or more precisely, the lack of it – can become a big problem. Cash flow issues are one of the main causes of business failures. Basically, if more money is flowing out of your business than is coming in, you end up without the resources to pay your staff or operating expenses.

In other words, you go bust.

Under the knife

In a crisis you will need to act fast to protect your cash. But do not panic and blindly slash spending across the board. This may feel as though you are acting decisively but you can do more long-term damage than the crisis itself.

Your overriding priority is to ensure the business survives, of course, but ideally you want to emerge stronger after the crisis, not so weak that your company ends up prey to opportunistic competitors. Bluntly, you want to be the opportunistic competitor.

So, despite the adrenaline, fear and uncertainty that a crisis triggers, my advice when making cuts is to use a scalpel, not an axe. At Argonon, we call this process open-heart surgery because it is that serious, painful and necessary for survival.

Please don't try to do all this yourself. The pressure in a crisis is intense. Ask your Cobra team, your war cabinet, for advice and reach out to your peers for ideas and support.

The open-heart surgery is a purposeful, objective and inevitable process with a beginning, a middle and an end. First up, take a long, cold, hard look at your business and understand your current cash position. Face up to best- and worst-case scenarios. Adjust your budgets accordingly. You are going to make tough choices.

Determine what costs are discretionary and cut all of this spend. Eliminate all unnecessary expenses and spend only on what keeps you operational and generates revenue. Don't forget that essential spending may also include items that are critical for maintaining team morale or relationships with key customers or suppliers.

In the pandemic of 2020, I felt it was essential that I took an immediate pay cut. As a leader, I could not inflict pain on the business without taking my own fair share of it. As a result, a number of my colleagues did the same. Some negotiated pay delays – and they recouped their pay cut at a later date. Some decided not to take a pay cut at all. I accepted all of these decisions.

You must get a clear picture of where your cash is being spent – at every single level. You need to have control over every penny leaving your bank account.

During Covid, we asked our finance teams to go through every single budget line with each of the eight companies at Argonon and also all of the central operations departments like legal, finance and HR. We left no stone unturned. It was a microscopic process that took two long weeks.

Everything that could be cut was cut.

Most people were sanguine and realized that what we were doing was right. We did it collaboratively and with a lot of open conversation. But here comes the commitment – the hard end of the Flexible Method. There would be no exceptions. Every part of the business would be handled equally.

Shirley Escott, COO Leopard USA, recalls how difficult it was:

'There were hard decisions to make as we had to become a leaner production unit and that meant inevitable lay-offs and several regulars were not re-hired. I believe we acted with compassion but there was unhappiness as several members of the team had worked for Leopard USA for many years. This also led to insecurity for remaining members of staff and required Teams meetings to give everyone the chance to express their concerns and fears.'

Of course, we had some push-back. We felt particularly bad about having to lay off our valued freelancers. In the US, we made sure we could guarantee one extra month from March 2020 to April 2020 to give our team access to one more month's medical insurance. And we sought out every possible support scheme from government. More on this in Chapter 12.

It was heartbreaking. Losing your people will be the most painful part of the open-heart surgery. There is just no getting around that. We are a close-knit group and it hurt. What we did was promise we would do everything in our power to get people back into work as soon as we could. We have kept that promise.

Our average headcount for Argonon was higher in 2021 than in 2020. So we really managed to maintain our staffing levels by utilizing the furlough scheme to keep people's jobs safe and bring people back.

In April 2020, 34 per cent of our staff were furloughed. By October 2020 this had fallen to 1 per cent, so were able to keep our promise of getting our staff back to work. I was delighted not to permanently lose colleagues, not just on a personal level – in our business, talent is at a premium and I don't want them to be poached by competitors.

Prioritize profit

To prioritize cash flow, focus on services that generate the most profit. Be prepared to let go of the least profitable areas that may be costing too much money.

Laura Bessell, Chief Operating Officer, Argonon, speaks about her process:

'My priority in terms of protecting our cash during Covid was to look at areas of the business that we'd already addressed as struggling and were waiting to see if they were going to perform and pull round. As soon as the pandemic hit, it was those areas that we had to really deal with immediately. If they couldn't have survived pre-Covid it was unlikely they were going to survive through the next period.

'Another key issue was cost control. We're always careful about this but it suddenly became a massive issue. We went through our cash, our liabilities, what would happen if we didn't do this or that for three months, and tried to model various scenarios, as well as working with some of the other units on basic project cost controls, so that we could see where staff weren't being fully utilized. And we spoke to the bank in the first week with our re-forecast and made sure they were on board and were going to support us.

'In terms of suppliers, we started contracting new suppliers in different ways, negotiating a different payment schedule so that if we had to shut down, we weren't exposed for a lot of cash up front.'

Laura introduced staggering our payments, paying people later and paying more on delivery, building all sorts of get-out clauses into the contracts so we were less likely to lose cash on things when we went into lockdown again. We paid the studio fees only when we were sure we could go ahead with the shoot. With crew, we made sure we could stand down freelance people very quickly so that if we weren't able to shoot, our losses would be minimized as far as possible. When a shoot involved a lot of travelling, we looked at how we could use local crews rather than flying teams out to cut costs.

Sweat the small stuff

You must also deal with every single item of expenditure on processes, materials, services. Again, you will need your microscope and scalpel – and people on your team who are willing to go deep.

Susie Field, former General Manager, Argonon, had plenty of experience with this in 2008:

'Going back to the Credit Crunch, we also went through everything with a fine-tooth comb and everything non-essential was cut. We thought carefully about who could use cabs. We had this big thing about stationery. Each time a new production manager came in they would order a lot of it and we said no, we're going to stop all that. We went round the building and collected all the staplers and emptied all the drawers. They were full of boxes of stuff. I said, right, we don't need any more staples for the next five years. And people were like, how can it matter? But it was all those little things adding up together.'

Our staff thought we were going over the top and couldn't imagine that minuscule everyday purchases would have any effect, but uncontrolled spending can really add up. Have you ever totted up uncontrolled spending on 'trivial' items? You may be surprised and see that you need to control small-scale spending as well as cap bigger purchasing in a crisis. We call them critical non-essentials.

Tightening up

Identify areas of waste or unnecessary expense in your operations. Scrutinize all service contracts and subscriptions and cancel those that aren't absolutely necessary to daily operations or strategic goals.

In a major crisis we have found that it is worth trying to negotiate better terms with debtors and creditors. Review supplier contracts and negotiate more favourable terms if possible. Leverage relationships with key suppliers to renegotiate contracts with better pricing and terms. Ask if you can delay any payments during the crisis. If they can't or won't help, consider switching to new suppliers.

In turn, you may need to help key customers who are in trouble by altering their payment terms. This will preserve goodwill in the long term.

Communicate honestly with your main internal and external stakeholders to dispel any uncertainty about what's going on, and continue to do so. This will help protect important relationships and retain goodwill.

Engage your team and communicate how they contribute to the recovery. Avoid sugar-coating and be honest and transparent about the choices you are making and the reality of the situation. People will respond better to you being straight with them. Try to be optimistic about the future and kindle hope. The crisis will pass.

You may want to consider switching staff to part-time roles where possible. Working from home will save on office costs and utilities.

It goes without saying that you should delay or cancel non-essential projects. Right now, the top priority is bringing in cash and keeping the business going. Look at ways of speeding up the flow of cash into your business. Perhaps you can ask customers for an up-front deposit or partial payment rather than billing them for the full amount after the services or products have been delivered.

Instead of waiting until the end of the month, invoice immediately after delivery of the products or services. You may also be able to invoice to cover services delivered to date. Don't forget to chase up those debts too. We have someone who has the perfect balance of politeness and firmness on the phone.

Optimize processes to eliminate waste and improve general organizational efficiency. You may find you can make savings through efficiencies and automation. This could be the perfect time to accelerate that switch to new technology and transformative initiatives. Repetitive and time-consuming tasks should be top of your list for automation.

It's worth remembering that even in a crisis, companies do need to spend money in order to make it. Consider borrowing if necessary. Get all the public and private funding and support that is available – I'll go into this more in Chapter 12.

Cash in the attic?

A crisis is an opportunity to look in your storeroom to see if there is anything in there that can be sold, repurposed or brought back to life. Are there any non-essential business assets you could sell?

Basically, you can channel Marie Kondo. Look at everything in your storeroom and instead of asking yourself, does this bring me joy?, ask, does this bring me cash? If it's a no, then you should probably give it to charity or bin it and save yourself money and space on storage fees.

There is nothing like a crisis for a good clear-out.

Laura says:

'During Covid we were trying to find value in some of our existing assets. Market demand for content was higher because people weren't making new programmes. So it was obviously an opportunity because people were desperate for content. We saw that as a push to monetize our back catalogue. Some titles hadn't been picked up and we were able to sell and re-license them.'

During the Credit Crunch, filming was limited due to advertising budget cuts, so we looked to see if there was any way we could repurpose material we already had. *Missing Live* came out of that. This was a BBC One television series following the work of the police and the charity Missing People, as they search for some of the 210,000 people who are reported missing every year in the UK.

Susie remembers how resourceful they had to be:

'We took the documentary series Missing *and turned it into a live show, which was much cheaper to shoot. We put our presenters into a tiny old MTV studio. We took the model of the format and used filmed reconstructions of individual missing persons cases, live studio interviews with the friends and family of missing people and on-air appeals.'*

This show went on to be commended in the House of Commons as a programme that changed people's lives.

During Covid, to bring cash in we looked at other old ideas that we could revive. *Cash in the Attic* is a show that helps you find hidden treasures in your home and then sells them for you at auction. This daytime favourite originally ran on BBC One between 2002 and 2012, with over 500 episodes broadcast, and it sold in 167 countries. There are also several international versions. It occurred to me that the show might just work again.

Everybody was stuck in their home in lockdown, so could we possibly film them there while preserving their safety? Everybody was struggling for cash – might they welcome the idea of liquidating some assets? It is also what we call a wish fulfilment show – it makes people feel good. Could the time be right to revive it?

I rewrote the concept, with help from my colleagues in LA who came at it with fresh eyes, and we sold it to HGTV and Discovery+. We pitched it again and it was picked up by Channel 5 in the UK for a run of 40 episodes. We are now going to turn it into a gaming app as well – another example of an opportunity emerging from a crisis.

Capitalize on all existing assets

Are there any assets just sitting in your real or metaphorical attic or storeroom that could be monetized?

Have you ever managed to revive assets, ideas or skills to bring in the cash? Sometimes you may not even realize you have these assets.

During the pandemic, Walmart, the world's second largest retailer, grew e-commerce sales by 90 per cent. Like other big retailers such as eBay, Target and Kroger, Walmart is now grossing billions in sales by monetizing an asset in their 'storeroom' – customer data.

The US digital consulting company Publicis Sapient reports that another giant grocery chain boosted digital sales by 225 per cent from its customer data platform (CDP) in the first three quarters of 2020.

By creating their own media networks to utilize information on customers' buying behaviour, retailers can channel products or offers to them based on knowledge acquired at the point of sale and by analysing media impressions to provide deeper insights into their customers' purchasing intent and journey.

The urgency of the crisis forced these companies to mine their assets and in doing so accelerated a development that will now be a mainstay of future retailing.

So digging out your cash in the attic may not only get you through the emergency, it may also help open up a profitable future post-crisis.

Have you considered looking through your database of clients to see how you might engage more deeply with them? You will doubtless have more depth and value in your clients, your storeroom and your catalogue than you know.

It is remarkable how our history can be there for us in times of need. Do not overlook the power of your past to inform and guide you in the present. Let's now look at how you can fire up the past to boost your present and future.

The Flexible Method tools – Protect your cash

▶ Fully grasp your current cash position
▶ Identify and eliminate all unnecessary expenses
▶ Employ efficiencies and automation
▶ Talk to your debtors, creditors and bank
▶ Negotiate flexible terms with suppliers
▶ Repurpose older ideas and assets

CHAPTER SEVEN

Learn from history

I don't know where it came from, but I have a deep-seated belief that things happen for a reason and make us stronger.

My dad and mum gave me the best they could: a safe home, food, a good education, love. They were generous gifts and I am thankful for them. Dad was an intellectual and an alcoholic and struggled with his demons. Both my parents had their limitations in how far they were able or willing to connect with me emotionally. At school and then through life, I had my share of knocks. Some of it was traumatic and I only truly found myself when I left home and went away to university to mix with a broad and diverse crowd.

One of the biggest gifts those early years gave me was a determination to adapt and survive. I had to learn to defend myself from attack – verbal, emotional, intellectual and physical – build a strong and resilient base starting with my life partnership and then nurture a team around me of kind, intelligent, worldly and honest friends, allies and advisors. Some of growing up was painful but it made me strong.

I now thank the adversity and the difficult times for giving me the tools to become a happy and successful adult.

You may have also overcome challenges in life. Do you remember how you felt? How, after the dust settled, you started to see more clearly and could put together an exit strategy? Did you learn from that experience? Did it change the way you did things next time? This is the essence of human survival.

I apply these same principles in my business.

When disaster strikes, crises can feel unprecedented, but very little is truly unprecedented. A knowledge of past crises helps put current situations into context.

As business leaders we already have a growing list of 21st-century disasters from which we can draw lessons: Covid, SARS, recessions, terrorist atrocities, wars and natural disasters among them. Big shocks to a major economy's financial system often catch people unprepared, but severe, painful recessions occur every decade.

Looking back is healthy. It provides comfort that this crisis will pass, that people coped once and will probably cope again. It should also provide ideas on how you should prepare this time around. Who did things right in the past? And who made mistakes we can avoid? There is a rich resource of wisdom through learning from the past – if you are receptive to it.

Crunch time

The great recession of 2008 was a hell of a shock to the system and a real wake-up call. The global banking crisis was triggered by packaging US sub-prime mortgages with low-risk ratings. Banks lost money and became reluctant to lend. It became difficult for firms and consumers to borrow from banks, leading to plummeting demand.

It was the most serious financial crisis since the Great Depression of the 1930s and the ensuing recession led to the loss of more than $2 trillion from the global economy. Most economists didn't see it coming and governments were unprepared when it struck.

I am a fervent knowledge gatherer. I subscribe to a dozen news outlets and websites and read voraciously. I like to get a sense of everything that is being said out there in the big wide world and then pick through the morass to try to find the heart of the matter. Over the holidays at the turn of 2007–8 it was clear that the severity of the ensuing recession threatened the survival of societies. There were riots, rising extremism and populism, and runs on the banks.

Consumer spending fell. The TV industry was hit badly by cancelled subscriptions and a sharp drop in advertising revenue, resulting in deep cuts to staff and budgets. Networks stopped commissioning new shows. If we don't win commissions, we have no income. No income means no business. It is that simple.

Like many others, my company was faced with ruin. At the time, people were even talking about the end of capitalism. How were we going to survive?

I was bracing myself to talk to my team – from what business leaders were saying I knew that in such a crisis, the first thing to do is communicate with your staff and protect them. Do everything humanly possible to keep your people.

As we returned from the holidays on 5 January 2008, I called a meeting with my whole team. I remember vividly walking into our board room, everyone assembled, anxious and expectant faces on me. I welcomed them back to work and empathized with them about the shocking impact of the Credit Crunch and how it was going to affect us. And then I got to the most important bit – I said we were committed to keeping EVERY SINGLE ONE of our talented team. Everybody must stay, no lay-offs. BUT we were going to have agree to tighten our belts, not recruit anyone new for a while, and it would be all hands on deck.

Everything that needed to be done – researching ideas, writing pitches, shooting, editing – would be done by us. We would bring in no outside help or freelance support as we would normally. We would roll up our sleeves and do it ourselves. Some office-based executives would temporarily have to step down a level and get back out on the road to film, producers might have to jump into the edit, editorial assistants would need to help across several different projects at once.

We would need to increase our creativity and productivity by 25 per cent (i.e. devise more, bigger, better projects), super-serve our existing clients and seek out new ones. If we did this together, I told them, we had a chance of surviving.

Susie Field, former general manager, Argonon, recalls what a frightening time it was:

'I was terrified that everyone was going to lose their homes. I was at the back of the room when James came in and spoke to us. What he did really well was he identified our biggest fear. What's the worst that could happen? A lot of people would lose their jobs and we would be left to somehow finish 115 episodes of Cash in the Attic *with no staff. That was the absolute worst.*

'James said he would executive produce it and I would be production manager. We'd just step in and do the production roles ourselves. Just make it happen. And while we were making it happen, things would hopefully settle down and we'd carry on delivering brilliant shows.

'He said we'd all have to step down a level and do other jobs, maybe do things that are outside of your job description, and we weren't going to be grand about it because by doing it we can keep as many people employed as we possibly can.'

After addressing the worst-case scenario and accepting it could happen, I said okay, working back from that, how do we get to where we need to be to at least limit the damage?

Back to Susie:

'There was the odd bit of "Well I'm not putting up with this" that you get in any company. But I think generally speaking the key people in the company who were loyal to the brand and who loved their jobs, who loved coming to work every day, they were the people that really stepped up and made it work.

'I think it's really important for the big chief to be present in some shape or form and the message always has to be, look, we know what we're doing. I've got a brilliant team working for me. They all know where we're going. Give us some time and we'll get this sorted out.

'Where there's good communication, there is a lot of trust. It reassures people and ensures that things happen. When you've had a long-term commitment to building that sort of network of relationships and when a crisis does happen, you've got a lot of deep-rooted communication in place.'

I have already stressed the importance of communicating clearly, frequently and frankly while presenting a calm and purposeful plan of action. When we were hit by a second existential crisis in 2020 – the Covid-19 emergency – our experience during the 2008 crisis was an invaluable source of learning. In fact, we would probably have fared far worse had we not come through the Credit Crunch and survived. It meant we had the experience to respond quickly to protecting our cash, communicating with our team and adapting.

The Flexible Method was born during the Credit Crunch and has been refined during many other crises over the years. Too many.

Terror on the tube

More sinister disasters that impact businesses are terrorist attacks.

On 7 July 2005, Islamist suicide bombers with rucksacks full of explosives attacked central London, killing 52 people and injuring hundreds more.

Terrorist attacks in London and New York came as a profound shock to our staff, especially to younger members of our teams who had not experienced such horrors before. Older managers who had grown up during the IRA bombing campaign were able to draw on their experience of numerous atrocities to help steady nerves and offer calm and compassionate leadership.

This is not the main reason that I advocate a truly diverse workforce – which includes having people in your team from every decade (we have people in their teens and in their seventies) – but maturity and a steady hand of experience have huge value.

This depth of knowledge certainly helped us steady the ship. Susie Field remembers:

'The streets were basically silent, except for sirens of emergency vehicles going up and down. I got on a train at Waterloo and people were covered in soot from the bombing. I never thought, this is the end of London. I never thought, oh my God, this is the start of something terrible. I always had absolute faith in this being one of a number of incidents of terrorist attacks that I was going to live through.

'I think that came from being a young person during the IRA bombs in London in the Seventies and that being so much part of our school life, bomb scares and people being shot and the local pub being blown up. So I was never worried about that. I was worried about people's mental health and later that day sent out emails saying, we understand that this is a frightening time, but we have taken government advice and it is business as usual. If you can come in, please try to come in and then we'll all be here together.

'We wanted people to feel safe. And I think that we thought that people feel safest when they're in their routines. And we wanted people to know that if they wanted to talk about anything, they could.

'People who had been on one of the bombed trains came in and were very upset. They were very shaken up by the whole thing. I remember sitting in my office with people and saying, do you want to talk about it? Are you comfortable? What do you want to do? And most people just wanted to just get on, get things done and not have a drama. We just thought right, sod them, we're just going to get on with it. And we came back and just got on with it.'

Susie was able to draw on her experiences from history to put people first, demonstrate calm leadership, communicate with her team and care for their mental health. All elements of the Flexible Method.

Have you ever been able to draw on your experiences during a crisis? Unpleasant as they are, have you found that they made you more resilient to future shocks?

Building resilience

During the Covid pandemic, public health experts were able to draw knowledge from the most recent SARS and MERS epidemics. This showed the effectiveness of wearing face masks, physical distancing, washing hands and good ventilation. These measures saved many lives.

Looking further back, data from the Spanish flu pandemic of 1918–20 (which despite its name started in Kansas) showed that quick, short and strict lockdowns were most effective in containing the spread of the disease. Scientific studies found that US cities that acted earliest and most forcefully, like St Louis which imposed a near-total lockdown within two days of its first case, had lower peak death rates than cities that started late, such as Philadelphia. This knowledge helped inform policy makers during Covid.

Like recessions and epidemics, natural disasters also regularly cause business disruption. To enhance its resilience and mitigate the impact of disasters, Walmart has instigated effective disaster planning and preparation that enables the retailer to continue to serve customers after extreme weather events such as hurricanes.

Although climate change is making storm intensity and frequency more unpredictable, Walmart uses data from previous storms to predict customer and community needs and to know where to direct necessary supplies and personnel. In 2020 the hurricane season was predicted to be extremely active. Walmart acted weeks in advance to ship water and essential items near coastal areas to reduce response times.

Holidays in hell

Access Travel Management has become expert at responding to such disasters. Part of their job is to transport film crews and journalists around the world, ensuring they are safe. The company's media clients have already been disrupted by Islamist terror attacks in London, Manchester, Berlin and Paris and most recently the terrible war in Ukraine.

In times of peace, looking after their clients requires a big logistics effort. In times of crisis, a whole new approach is needed. Disaster recovery plans have been developed based on past experience. As well as terror attacks, the teams rehearse for crises such as power cuts and natural disasters. The plans are updated with every incident.

When a crisis suddenly overturns travel and accommodation plans, Access sets up emergency response teams drawn from a pool of 30 people to look after hundreds of clients. They monitor press output and social media reports in real time to advise clients on the ground what to do, checking with accommodation providers in the immediate vicinity of a terror attack to see if those businesses are operating. As well as looking to extract people at risk, they send news crews to hotspots to cover the story.

Lee Gunn, Operations Director, Access Travel Management, considers how they changed their approach:

'We have learned a lot of lessons on how to respond quickly and support and protect our clients as we've already seen how things unfolded in the past. For instance, our team reassures clients that we've spoken to the hotel and that they are open and willing to accept their reservation. It's part of the very practical, client-focused information that allows people to go about their business amid the disruption and uncertainty.

'With Ukraine we had advance warning of the invasion due to the build-up of Russian troops so we didn't need to set up an immediate emergency team, but still used our expertise with accommodation for journalists, asking things like, does the hotel have an underground basement, car park or whatever that is going to give some bomb protection for guests?'

Have you ever considered booking into a hotel and checking first that it has a bomb shelter? Me neither.

Access have certainly learned from history and their customers appreciate it. Lee adds: *'We have seen a phenomenal response to this work from our clients.'*

Critical thinking

Although you can use elements learned from one disaster in a current crisis, critical thinking is still crucial in order to respond effectively. I would encourage you to use the core elements of the Flexible Method – listen, ask questions, be open-minded, willing to change your thinking. And then once you have decided your course of action, act with total commitment.

When disaster strikes, your first priority is to get your people to safety. With your bravest thinkers at your side, lead calmly and purposefully and step up your communication with your team.

To save your business, stop all unnecessary expenditure, cut carefully and mine existing assets to bring in cash.

Taking on board lessons of the past will help you constructively plan the future.

Implementing these measures saved our businesses, so I am glad to have had the opportunity to share them with you. I've outlined many of the measures we implemented during the Credit Crunch and Covid and highlighted some other learnings from disasters such as the New Zealand earthquake and the terrorist attacks across Europe.

Having been through so many disasters, I think we can all count ourselves as seasoned survivalists. The experience and learnings we are still distilling will prove invaluable tools in the future.

Crises evolve and the time will come when you should turn your focus away from the first response of firefighting and begin steering your organization through the maelstrom. Let's turn to some of the tools which will help you navigate this next critical part of the journey.

The Flexible Method tools – Learn from history

▶ Look at lessons from the past to think constructively about the future
▶ Be open to thinking flexibly and even changing your mind
▶ Critical thinking is crucial – adapt solutions to the present day

PART 3

Steering through a crisis

CHAPTER EIGHT

Hold onto your values

'I have to sleep at night'

On 2 November 2020, on the eve of the Trump–Biden presidential election in the US, a politician in Oklahoma wrote: 'Vote for decency. Vote for empathy, honesty, competence, thoughtfulness, integrity, compassion, humility, civility, dignity, obligation, inclusion, love, selflessness, service, courage & aspiration. Vote for virtues that will rebuild & reunify our nation.'

No prizes for guessing which candidate this politician was endorsing (Twitter, 2020). What is surprising is that in this red state, this was written by a Republican – David Holt, mayor of Oklahoma City.

When interviewed about his speech, Mayor Holt gave this insight:

'I thought about these words for many weeks. I would say it is pretty reflective of what I consider to be core values of an elective leader in America. So to me, if I were trying to make a list, I don't think I would do any better than that of the values and virtues that I think an elected leader should have.'

David Holt is clearly not your average Republican. After he was elected in 2018 as the youngest mayor of a major US city at the age of 39, he launched a billion-dollar investment initiative to make Oklahoma City somewhere that people with disposable income, job creators, want to live. This seems to be working: the city now has historically low unemployment, record sales tax and double the national population growth.

In 2019, Holt's focus switched to boosting inclusivity, establishing centres for people with mental health issues, domestic violence victims, young people, civil rights and former criminal offenders.

'This is to ensure that everything we're doing is not just for upper middle class and above. That was a priority for a long time and we came a long way on that, but then it was time to make sure that we're taking care of everybody.

'My whole motto as mayor, my whole mantra, is 'One OKC'. It's a unifying message. As we move forward, it's also about making sure that it's a city that has a heart, and with compassion that's ensuring that everybody has equal opportunity.

'In America, it seems to be very easy and very tempting to let go of quite a few of your values when you are serving in elected office because you're trying to stay there and it can seem as if the priorities of the public are ever changing and it must be your obligation to change with them if you want to stay in office. To some degree, of course, you have to be responsive to your electorate, but you also have to remember, you're a leader for a reason.

'I can adapt, but I cannot simply become a different person. I cannot prioritize being reelected or climbing a ladder above all else, including my core values. And certainly that philosophy was tested as Donald Trump rose into power.

'I have to sleep at night. I would much rather be proud of my service on my deathbed than be proud of the length of my service.'

The Covid-19 pandemic could have been a good excuse for Mayor Holt to ditch his inclusivity programme but he held his values and continued to promote them.

In the 2022 mayoral elections, voters recognized his stance by returning him to office with a landslide. He is living proof that you can hold onto your values and come out a winner.

Core values

Mayor Holt describes how he was guided by his core values. They are the guiding light that show your team and your clients what you are like as a company and how you behave in your work environment. They are principles that give a company a greater purpose.

Core values cut across all departments of your business and can unify otherwise separate entities, bringing the whole together. This will improve your output and help you make better decisions as an organization.

A workforce that shares common goals and objectives and is aligned in this way will bring more to their work. This will give you a competitive edge, enhance your position in the marketplace and make you stronger.

According to WordStream by LOCALiQ (WordStream, nd), an online source of digital marketing data:

▶ more than 63 per cent of consumers prefer to purchase brands with purpose
▶ highly engaged employees can increase performance by 200 per cent
▶ a culture that attracts high-calibre employees can lead to a 33 per cent revenue increase.

If you want your business to be strong enough to weather any storm, and have more clients, a happier and engaged team and make more money, core values count.

There isn't a set rule on how many core values you should have, but the key is to be authentic. Also, I think it is best to be concise so your team can remember your values easily.

Here are some examples.

ADIDAS

Performance: sport is the foundation for all we do and executional excellence is a core value of our Group.

Passion: passion is at the heart of our company. We are continuously moving forward, innovating and improving.

Integrity: we are honest, open, ethical and fair. People trust us to adhere to our word.

Diversity: we know it takes people with different ideas, strengths, interests and cultural backgrounds to make our company succeed. We encourage healthy debate and differences of opinion.

H&M

We believe in people
We are one team
Straightforward and open-minded
Keep it simple
Entrepreneurial spirit
Constant improvement

VIRGIN AIRLINES

We think customer
We lead the way
We do the right thing
We are determined to deliver
Together we make the difference

Cost-consciousness

Core values should be a mix of those that describe your company as it is now as well as what it strives to be. They should celebrate but also motivate; evoke pride but also inspire action. Core values are essential principles that guide your most important decisions.

I have drawn up some steps that I hope will help you to define your organization's core values:

Step 1 Put together a team: this process is all about engagement by the widest group of voices in your company. Be sure to bring together employees with very different perspectives in the business and from all levels.
Step 2 Brainstorm: allow your team to discuss what is important to them, what excites them, what motivates them.

Playing with words is going to be important here. They might include some of the following:

Agile	Consistent
Authentic	Courageous
Bold	Dependability
Compassionate	Experimentation

Expertise	Philanthropy
Fair	Pragmatic
Generous	Reliability
Honesty	Resilience
Inclusivity	Respect
Integrity	Simple
Justice	Speed
Kind	Sustainable
Mindful	Systemization
Open-minded	Teamwork
Original	Tenacious
Patience	Thorough
Perfection	Tolerant

Step 3 Define your top choices: this will take a while, so give yourselves plenty of time. I would recommend you choose two to five core values. When uncovering your core values, make sure each and every one of them is as strong and necessary as the next one.

Step 4 Roll it out: it is important that your whole team is on board with your core values. I would recommend inviting them to a group session where you can share your findings and then discuss them as a group. You may find this helps to sharpen your wording and your top selected core values.

Bring your values to life

After defining your values and sharing them with your team, it is time to let people know who you are and what you stand for. So, shout about it!

Your core values should be prominent on your company website, branding, literature and documentation. I would also ensure they become part of everyday processes in the business, including in your email signatures, recruitment interviews, onboarding and appraisals. You might even consider holding annual awards based on your values, nominated and voted for by the widest group.

Values can set your organization apart from the competition by clarifying its identity and uniting employees around something they really buy into.

Your values will play a big role in the quality of people you hire and who is attracted to your organization. Some people are just not going to be able to live up to your corporate values and will be better off elsewhere.

If a random member of your team was asked what your corporate values were, would they be able to recite them? To circulate them and make them part of the DNA of your corporate culture, your values need to be made clear and repeated. The more clarity you have about your core values, the more comfortable you will be about the decisions you take in a crisis and the more confident you will be in those values.

Your compass

A crisis can bring your values into sharp focus. Strong and meaningful values should provide a clear guide for how employees should behave. Empty values statements just spread cynicism and lower morale, undermining your credibility and distancing customers.

This book is all about making your business more resilient in a crisis and I believe your values will help you achieve this by clarifying what really matters. They also boost your personal resilience when you are undergoing huge levels of stress that impede your ability to think clearly. They will help guide you and make smart decisions. And if your values are understood and embraced by your entire team, they will help everyone in the organization make the right choices.

Whether you are aware of them or not, you will already have a set of personal core values that have helped guide you through life. Clarifying your own core values can make life's key choices feel easier. One of mine is 'be kind'. When I am not sure what to do, remembering this value helps me make the right choice – even if it means I suffer inconvenience or short-term financial loss. I was listed recently as one of the Top 50 Leaders of Kindness (cue angelic choir). But seriously, I was honoured to receive this listing and I got a lot of positive feedback for it.

The good news is that sticking to your values also pays off financially.

The US management consulting firm Bain & Company found that companies with a strong internal compass are 3.7 times more likely to be business performance leaders (Berman and Thurkow, 2020).

Knowing your core values is crucial to your authentic, effective leadership style.

Do you remember a time you had to make a very tough decision at a time of great stress and uncertainty? Wouldn't it have been helpful to feel secure in making that decision because you knew you were being true to your solid core values?

What is your company's purpose and what are its core values? I would encourage you to take time to reflect on this with your executives.

Trust is priceless

Remember that even in crisis situations not everything comes down to the traditional metrics of profit and loss. Is there anything more important than the trust you have from customers, employees and stakeholders?

Although your instinct may be to ditch values and culture and focus on the bottom line, a crisis is when they matter the most, even though you can't easily put a price tag on them – and even at the expense of short-term profits. This may sound too idealistic but losing trust will end up costing you more over time.

Business is based on trust. It takes years to build up a trusting relationship with your employees and customers. Many companies espouse values such as integrity, teamwork, ethics, transparency, customer satisfaction, innovation.

Trust builds reputation. In the words of *Forbes*: in business, your reputation is the only currency that matters (Walter 2014).

Sacrificing your values, your trust, your reputation as soon as the going gets tough shows everyone you didn't really believe in them in the first place. They were just weakly held aspirations. And as a result, your credibility collapses.

I am sure you can think of politicians who damaged their reputation after breaking promises. I'm also sure you don't want to join their ranks.

Values, trust and reputations matter.

During the Covid pandemic there were some companies that dropped their values. They were overwhelmed and felt that values could be disposed of as collateral damage.

Diversity

Let me share an example. In my industry, diversity and inclusion are a big problem. There are not enough people of colour working in the media. Not enough people from lower social economic backgrounds. Not enough people with disabilities. There is a lot of work that needs to be done.

As producers of television content, we have access to millions and millions of people every day – through handsets, tablets and TVs in living rooms and bedrooms. It is a very intimate relationship, with enormous power. I take this responsibility very seriously. It's our job to reflect the society we live in, represent the voices of everybody and engage with the widest possible community. If we fail to do this, we're not doing our job properly – and our content will be irrelevant.

We run an annual campaign called 'Argonon for Everyone'. We took a lot of professional guidance and we count our people annually – we want to make sure we have a healthy balance of women and men in senior leadership roles, and have set targets for people of colour, LGBTQI+, lower social economic backgrounds and disability, both visible and invisible. We want to ensure that Argonon is truly representative of the world we live in.

The murder of George Floyd in the middle of Covid was a deeply shocking event (BBC, 2020). I felt compelled to respond as leader of Argonon. We were going to deepen our commitments, not let them slide.

With backing from my HR team and 30 volunteers from across the Argonon Group in the UK and the US, we set up a new Diversity and Inclusion Committee. We all met online and wow, it was such a relief to be talking with this interesting group about something other than the pandemic.

Over the course of several meetings, we decided that our approach should be targeted. We agreed we would prefer a small number of concrete results rather than endless talk. So we set up four sub-committees. The first would look at how to get school-age pupils engaged with a career in the media. We teamed up with Speakers for Schools, a non-profit that specializes in under-18s, and sent some of our senior executives to talk with them. It was a great success.

The second group paired up with PACT, the Producers Alliance for Cinema and Television, a body that represents the independent sector of producers and distributors. It runs highly structured apprenticeships with a particular emphasis on diversity and inclusion. We signed up to take two interns, funded for an initial six months. We had to demonstrate not just willingness but also time and resources. We now have two salaried interns working for us in Liverpool and London.

The third group focused on mentoring and we paired with ScreenSkills, a body that helps run mentoring schemes. We established a formal mentoring scheme across our organization to promote and develop our existing team up the ladder. Many senior execs agreed to mentor a member of staff, me included. It is a very rewarding thing to do.

And the fourth group was US focused and committed to internship programmes on the East and West coasts. The specialist non-profits Streetlight in LA and Made in NY in New York helped us find and plan structured internships for two candidates. Again, we recruited one salaried intern on each coast and both have gone on to develop interesting careersin the media.

We pursued all of these projects and have had considerable success in each. We also had a lot of positive feedback internally and externally. I received a number of internal emails from young staff thanking us for this work.

I shall not name a business I know that did the exact opposite of what we did. They shut down their diversity and inclusion work. It was regarded as too much to worry about when everything else was so hectic. Staff morale plummeted. The management lost the personal touch and put the bottom line over its people. I call it big corporation sickness. Their business dropped 30 per cent during Covid. I am certain that ditching their commitment to their stated values played a direct role in this.

By ramping up our diversity and inclusion work during the crisis, the message we gave to our teams was that we really care about this stuff; we hold onto our values even when things get bad. If we had ditched our values, I think our staff would have felt miserable.

Your reputation is on the line

Ditching a commitment to putting people first, for example, might earn you quick wins that can contribute to your short-term survival, but your staff and customers will perceive you as being inauthentic and their loss of trust will have long-term consequences. For years after the crisis your team and customers will remember the fact that you dropped the values you once proclaimed sacrosanct.

And don't think that you can abandon your core values even temporarily during a crisis. It may be tempting to go for a quick win and tell yourself that you'll get back to normal once things settle down, but people will judge you for your actions because your choices reveal what is truly important to you.

Remember, your reputation is on the line.

Conversely, standing by your values can earn you respect and loyalty as a leader that continue long after the crisis has passed.

Your actions will be judged after the crisis by your customers and your employees. Sticking to your values and putting people first will inspire loyalty. People remember how they were treated when they were at their most vulnerable.

Open Homes

It is possible to leverage your values to make a difference in the world. The world will remember you for it.

When hundreds of thousands of people were made homeless by Hurricane Sandy in 2012, a lady in Brooklyn named Shell emailed Airbnb offering to put up displaced New Yorkers for free. More than 1,400 hosts then did the same. Because of this act of humanity, Airbnb then created the disaster response tool, Open Homes.

The tool was activated again in 2019 to host people displaced by wildfires in California. People were desperate and homeless. Airbnb reached out to their community of hosts, asking established hosts if they had a space available. Many were local to the fires and keen to help. They listed their homes for free on the website, offering relief stays for people needing a home or bed. Airbnb waived all booking fees.

Now as part of Airbnb's ongoing crisis support, hosts are spontaneously invited to open their doors to people affected by disasters all over the world. Via its non-profit arm, Airbnb.org, they offer free, short-term housing to refugees fleeing trouble spots, including Syria, Venezuela and Afghanistan.

A great example of how holding on to your values can do good, make your staff feel proud and enhance the public image of your company.

Pain

Unfortunately, the consequences of sticking to your values can be hard. It's easy to do during the good times, but sticking to your values can be painful in a crisis:

▶ Your core values limit your freedom of action and constrain your behaviour.
▶ People will criticize you if you fall short of your stated values.
▶ Maintaining your values requires constant effort.
▶ You can lose out economically in the short term.

But sticking to values that your team can rally around will help you to come through the crisis stronger and more united. It doesn't mean you cannot make cuts or take tough options. In such cases, be transparent, sharing the unappetizing choices with your team.

Frankly, if you are not prepared to live up to your values, don't bother – you are better off not formulating and promoting them in the first place.

When you are faced with making a tough decision that could impact the survival of your company, ask yourself whether there is another choice you can make that doesn't compromise your values.

Moment of truth

A major crisis can be a moment of truth for your values, forcing you to examine whether you really believe in the things you claim. This is why you should choose the values you publicly state, wisely. Walk the walk. Your team will respect you for it. But they will also call you out (or leave) if they think you are being inauthentic.

Have you publicly stated your corporate values? About 80 per cent of Fortune 100 companies have. It's a zeitgeisty thing to do as companies try to look politically correct to appeal to Generation Z consumers and job applicants. But all too often those values are too broad and bland to really mean anything. Integrity, customer satisfaction and teamwork are great, but shouldn't they be a given in any business?

Climate emergency

In the middle of Covid, we decided to establish an Argonon Climate Action Group. We produce some of our shows using Albert, an industry-approved tool for measuring environmental impact. I am all for this. It will hold us to account.

We decided that our first step was a full audit of where we are now as an organization. We created a checklist of things we need to do:

▶ Try to get all of our production Albert-compliant.
▶ Create an internal group to share information on international crews to reduce flying.
▶ Analyse where our group pension schemes are investing (if fossil fuels, then we will need to change provider).

▶ Establish an electric car scheme to help staff purchase.
▶ Explore a future commitment to B Corp certification with a commitment to make business more ethical and sustainable.

One of my senior team agreed to lead the group and is banging the drum. As with our diversity work, we prefer small, concrete actions with actual results rather than endless empty talk.

A wide range of staff from across the droup, UK and US, volunteered to join. Again, it has been a relief to discuss important matters with my colleagues that are not just pandemic related.

You should be able to look back on your actions with pride as you steer your company through a crisis, not realize too late that you panicked and harmed people with knee-jerk responses based on fear.

Easing your customers' pain in a time of crisis will be remembered and bind you closer to them.

How you support your wider community will also impact how people perceive your brand. Connecting with this community is something we turn to next.

The Flexible Method tools – Hold onto your values

▶ Values are your compass – don't ditch them in a storm
▶ Establish and promote your organization's core values
▶ Choose your core values with care – set achievable objectives
▶ Values and trust are your reputation – protect them at all costs, especially in a crisis

---

CHAPTER NINE

Collaborate, connect

Janet Archer watched the seething torrents of brown water race along the gulley a mile from her family hog farm in Goldsboro, Wayne County, North Carolina, cutting off the road. Thankfully the flood didn't reach her farmlands but winds of over 100 mph had caused widespread damage across the state and record rains had dumped trillions of gallons of rainwater onto the countryside.

A disaster on this scale could spell calamity for family farms in the state. With many of the roads impassable, feed for pigs could soon run out, meaning they would starve. Farm hands stuck on site couldn't continue working around the clock without relief and fuel for the generators couldn't be resupplied.

Thankfully Janet had stocked up on essential supplies. From experience she knew they could be cut off for days due to debris and flooding on the roads. And although Janet was isolated, she knew she wasn't alone during this hurricane season. A newly implemented approach meant the situation commanders at the North Carolina Pork Council were monitoring the progress of the storm and were responding to calls for help from other hog farmers in the state.

A call had just come in from another farmer: *'I need more trucks because I'm going to have to evacuate this entire farm.'* The supplier replied: *'We're on our way.'*

Elsewhere in the state a municipality diverted a helicopter that normally services the hospital to one farm so they could rotate the staff there and make sure the animals were fed.

Janet smiled. *'That kind of thing didn't happen before.'* As a producer education and outreach officer at the North Carolina Pork Council, she helped establish this new approach.

North Carolina is one of America's top hurricane hotspots. In 1999 Hurricane Floyd left more than $3 billion in damage in the state. Dykes broke, spreading millions of gallons of fertilizer effluent across the area. After that, the state imposed regulations to stop it happening again.

The North Carolina pork industry also instigated a new shared ownership structure to mitigate and share risk, with high levels of collaboration between suppliers who own the animals and provide feed to the farmers, who in turn own the facilities, labour and land.

Get off my land!

Janet continues the story:

'Farmers don't love it when you tell them what to do when they've been doing it for 100 years. Telling them "You're doing this wrong" did not make any friends.

'When we brought in the federal and state inspections, it didn't start out great. Inspectors were worried about going onto a farm in case somebody was going to have a firearm or something.

'Animals still have to be fed, cared for, even during flooding and storms. By collaborating with each other, we were able to mitigate the effects for everybody.'

Instead of reacting on the eve of a hurricane, they start preparing well in advance.

'Now we're always watching what's happening everywhere, monitoring the development of weather systems around Africa. And we will immediately start preparing, topping up all of our feed bins, any containers that could hold feed in fact, because we don't know when a truck can get in there if we're isolated. Fuel for our generator is also filled to the brim days ahead because we don't know how long we may be without power.'

The new approach won over the farmers.

'Now there's a real sense of partnership. I would argue that we are better because of what happened in previous hurricanes. We are more resilient because of those regulations. We were operating in something of a silo. "These are my pigs, I'll take care of my pigs, you do what you need to do but I got my little pigs here."

'We are now much more collaborative. Not only with the state but with each other as farmers and suppliers.'

I admit I never thought of farmers as being particularly flexibly minded, but my impressions turned out to be pure hogwash after speaking with Janet. They prepared, learned from history and collaborated. All key elements of the Flexible Method. The members of the pork industry in North Carolina worked together, listened and improved their way of working, benefiting all the stakeholders.

Reach out

When the survival of your organization is threatened in a crisis, your natural instinct can be to focus on self-preservation. As you watch your income, savings and even essential supplies dry up, your anxiety urges you to protect what you have and guard it against others. You may think about how to ringfence your clients and hoard resources.

This is an understandable but unhelpful response. Effective collaboration, especially in a crisis, can boost long-term commercial success. It is also good for your health and wellbeing. It is a win–win.

If it doesn't come naturally to you to reach out to others, especially in an emergency, this is a key skill I urge you to develop. It is one of the backbones of the Flexible Method. As a leader, it is a tool to rely on. I also recommend you build collaboration into your corporate culture.

Harvard Business Review, the general management magazine, conducted research on the 2008 financial crisis (Gardner and Matviak, 2020). It found that collaboration leads to sustainably higher commercial performance. The most highly collaborative companies – the top 10 per cent – grew their business during the crisis and continued that upward trajectory afterwards. Those in the bottom 70 per cent hunkered down and dramatically reduced their collaboration with others. The revenue generated by this group contracted during the crisis and had still not recovered five years after the recession had ended.

How sad is that? People felt bad, shut themselves off and weakened themselves in the process in the long term.

The reasons for the success of the more collaborative companies is that reaching out to a wider group allows you to tap into different perspectives and experiences. This enables you to come up with new solutions and adapt dynamically to rapidly chang-ing, complex problems. Having a diverse workforce within your organization also increases your ability to problem solve.

Collaboration counters any natural tendency to just dig in. It will help you alleviate anxiety and give you hope. You must do everything to calm yourself from fear or you will become more risk averse and close down options for escape.

Collaborating externally will certainly help your organization if teamwork and collaboration are already embedded in your culture. Ways of encouraging this include listening to your teams, praising teamwork and having a higher sense of purpose that motivates people to think about the greater good and act collectively. You should also emphasize this sense of purpose when seeking to col-laborate with other organizations that may share your values.

Peer to peer

When disaster strikes, I recommend you look beyond your organ-ization for help. The first place to turn when widening your cir-cle externally is your sector or industry network. How are your peers responding? Are they facing similar problems? Is there something your industry or the government can do to help? If so, teaming up to create alliances will give you a stronger voice when lobbying.

During the pandemic I joined a cross-industry working group at PACT. I'd always been grateful to them for their work on our behalf but had never had much time to get involved. It was just one commitment too many in my schedule. But in the first lock-down in 2020, sitting at home in front of my computer, I had the urge to jump in. I picked up the phone and volunteered. I am so glad I did.

The first group I joined looked at how to get the whole industry back into production. We set up health and safety guidance and protocols to get film and TV productions back up and running safely where possible within the government's guidelines.

An industry taskforce was set up around the issue of insurance and calling on the government to set up a state-backed fund for productions that were unable to get cover because of the pandemic and its ongoing associated risks. PACT identified this as *the* critical issue to be resolved as quickly as possible because even if productions were able to go ahead within government guidelines, they might still be prevented due to a lack of insurance.

Argonon willingly shared all its detailed Covid protocols and listened and absorbed others' experiences. This is a constantly updating document, even now.

There was a real sense of intel sharing and cross-industry collaboration. It gave us all a common purpose and the feeling that we were not alone. It was reassuring and collegiate. It also paid off – we secured a government insurance scheme through industry pressure. This enabled us to restart production following strict health guidelines.

Collaboration can also make you a better leader. You may be surprised at how much you can learn from your peers. No matter what your problem is, the chances are someone else has already been through it, so surrounding yourself with people who can speak from experience is invaluable.

Good deeds

Neil Garfinkel is managing member of Abrams Garfinkel Margolis Bergson LLP, a law firm with 150 employees based in Los Angeles and New York. Its main business is real estate.

Many businesses struggled with the challenge of having to switch to remote working during lockdown, but Neil's mortgage-closing business faced a particular challenge. In New York, mortgage papers required for closing couldn't legally be signed electronically, on old-fashioned 'wet' signature was required.

Neil details the process:

'If you're buying a house, your attorney, the seller's attorney, the brokers and the title company would show up and everything would be done around the table: delivery of the deed ownership, lenders' documents and keys, etc. Now all of a sudden you can't do that. Hey, you can't even be in the room with someone.'

At the same time, interest rates were lowered to 0.5 per cent to stimulate the economy and overnight people were refinancing like crazy. The real estate market went nuts and instead of closing down for the duration of the pandemic, they were now having to cope with a massive property-buying revival.

It was exactly the opposite of what Neil had expected – a warning that you should keep on your toes as surprising twists do happen in a crisis.

To cope with the avalanche of refinance applications Neil had to hire 50 people during that time.

'To get papers signed our staff would get in their car, drop off closing documents and watch people sign through the window. It was pretty amazing. We did more closings in those two years than we ever did before. We're talking an enormous amount of closings.

'We thought, we've got to automate, we've got to go from wet signatures to electronic signatures.'

So, Neil's firm teamed up with the New York State Association of REALTORS trade association to ask the state governor to permit electronic notarization as an emergency order. This measure was adopted. Another example of what can be achieved by lobbying as well as how technological developments can accelerate during a crisis.

Instead of being overwhelmed and having to turn down valuable business during an unexpected boom, Neil and his erstwhile competitors got together to rush through a change in the law.

The Covid-19 pandemic saw unprecedented levels of cooperation all over the world. Competition regulators, in Europe and the US, lifted anti-trust restrictions to promote collaboration between competitors to help combat the impact of the pandemic. Competitor collaboration will also be needed as we face threats such as climate change and other global issues.

In a crisis, as well as collaborating with your competitors, you are going to need to think laterally about whether someone in your team has a skill or an asset that you can leverage (with their collaboration, of course).

After Ed Templeton's restaurant business was shut down by the Covid pandemic, he had to come up with some ideas fast to keep himself and his team afloat. His wife was also just pregnant for the first time, so there was no room for failure.

Ed identified his friend, chef Tom Straker, as a potential collaborator and they devised a new business together:

'Tom Straker has a big Instagram following, which expanded during the pandemic. We started a weekend click-and-collect setup. We would cook a dish every weekend during lockdown and post it as a video on Instagram. His followers could book a slot and come and collect their cacio e pepe or fish finger sandwich or pizza or whatever.

'We set up a kitchen in the entrance and they'd come to the front door during their slot, as we were basically cooking in the entrance. There was a table in the doorway. It was all paid for

online so we could just say hello, hand the food to them and off they'd go. And next thing we knew, we had 1,000 people turning up to our restaurant and buying this pre-prepared pasta dish to go.'

Friends in need! Ed could have put all his staff on furlough, shut up shop and sat at home, hoping the infection rate would eventually flatten enough for him to reopen. Instead, this collaboration boosted the number of covers they would have got normally and increased their profits on the food. A prime example of the key Flexible Method elements of thinking flexibly, adapting and collaborating, then following through the decision with utter commitment.

As well as collaborating with colleagues in your industry, many people found that working with direct competitors can bring surprising benefits.

Snap!

London-based portrait and events photographer Andy Sillett spent the Covid-19 pandemic photographing frontline medics on a voluntary basis, but as lockdown restrictions eased he began to get busy with bookings again.

'Another photographer contacted me and said, "We have similar clients and charge similar rates, we could cover for each other. No poaching clients, of course." My instinctive reaction was to not let a competitor anywhere near my customers, but one of the problems of being a sole trader is that you can't easily take holidays because if you turn down a job your customers will go elsewhere and you could lose them permanently.

113

'Working together to cover each other when we're double booked or on holiday now means we keep our customers happy and can balance out the lost fees from jobs we can't do.

'I don't think I would have agreed to share my customers with a competitor before the pandemic. Maybe attitudes to collaboration have changed because of the way people stepped up and helped others during Covid.'

Brexit bites

Tony Stanton is managing owner of Deep Blue Sea Training, a sea school in Majorca, Spain, training people to skipper boats. After navigating through the stormy waters of Covid, another massive blow came along. On 1 January 2021, after a year of transition, British citizens lost the freedom to travel and work in the European Union.

Tony sums up the problem:

'British maritime certifications are very highly regarded worldwide. It's very pragmatic, hands on, unlike here in Spain, where training is 99 per cent theoretical. Now the Spanish decide no British licences are valid in Spain any more and no British boats can function commercially in Spain.'

All of Tony's boats were forced out of action and he could not hire his core staff from the UK to run his courses.

As a Spanish resident with a work permit Tony managed to keep working by renting a Spanish boat with a Spanish skipper on board. It was an expensive solution and Tony was working 'unhealthily hard' to keep afloat.

'Then competitor schools started talking to one another,' he recalls. One of the people Tony collaborated with was Steve

Wickenden, a fellow British entrepreneur who lives in Mallorca, one of Europe's top yachting centres. An informal collaboration evolved.

'We'd just meet up every now and again over coffee and say, "Do you want to borrow my boat? Because I know you're stuck." It turned out to be really mutually beneficial.

'We were coming under lots of pressure as we were coming out of the pandemic, Mallorca was waking up, suddenly finding book-ings were up 30 per cent pre-Covid times and everybody wanted to go boating in Mallorca.

'One of us would complain about not being able to get a mooring and the other would say, "I might be able to help you. I know some guys who are doing this and that." Steve found me a home to put one of the boats and said, "I've got some people that'll help to clean it, and a maintenance guy. Maybe you should use my workshop." He was very generous with that.

'Had it not been for Brexit, would we have collaborated in that sense? No, I don't think so. Wouldn't have needed to. We'd have just gone and ploughed our own furrows. Steve's been doing his thing here for 20-odd years, I've been doing it here for nine. It's only now that we are doing this.'

Tony and Steve are still working well side by side. They now have more business than ever and Tony is able to work fewer hours to devote some time to his passion project – a radio station 'play-ing the coolest music between Mallorca and Ibiza'. The Flexible Method in action.

Collaboration isn't always as straightforward. It requires regu-lar communication, mutual trust and clear agreements, especially concerning intellectual property (IP) and liability. If you decide to deepen your new collaborations, this will need to be thought through in detail.

Connecting with customers

In normal times you usually connect externally through customer journeys and customer experience, but in an emergency the needs of your customers will suddenly change dramatically. They will feel scared, depressed and worried about how to keep their jobs or feed their families.

Putting people first and practising empathy – key elements of the Flexible Method – will allow you to care for your customers during a crisis, laying the foundations of lasting goodwill with communities.

A good place to start is to think about what your customers need right now and how you can help with your products or services. This may involve rapidly adapting your offering while still playing to your strengths.

Companies that help customers in financial difficulties gain trust, for example utility companies that did not cut off customers during the pandemic or entertainment companies and cultural organizations that provided free virtual content during lockdown.

Can you think of companies that reached out to you in your hour of need? How did that make you feel towards them? Can you imagine the amount a business would have to spend on marketing normally to achieve the same result?

Have you ever used an opportunity to support your customers and communities in a crisis? Did the connections this forged outlive the impacts of the crisis?

Connect with your community

Established in 1856 in Manchester, England, the Hallé Concerts Society is one of the world's oldest orchestras. Known internationally as the Hallé Orchestra, it is partly funded by the Arts Council but its core income comes from performing concerts.

This came to an abrupt end during Covid.

David Butcher, Chief Executive, the Hallé Concerts Society, was filled with dread: '*I really feared orchestras would not survive the pandemic.*'

Unable to perform live, the Hallé decided to strengthen its social care partnerships by organizing online concerts for people suffering from dementia or other kinds of mental illnesses. David says:

'*This music therapy may sound like a "nice-to-have" rather than an essential service, but people feeling that they can actually relax and enjoy themselves through singing and making music is scientifically proven to have beneficial effects in terms of how the brain develops and easing the progress of dementia.*

'*We also created an NHS choir, so nurses and doctors were able to sing together to escape the turmoil and pressures they were all suffering during the pandemic. They were performing well-known choral works – everything from Mozart to ABBA. We got feedback from the doctors and nurses just saying, "I've had the toughest time and so being able to sing and just escape from my day job has been a little bit of a lifesaver for me." But we've certainly found that as we're now coming out of this, the appetite is even stronger than it was before in terms of the importance of making music, just for health and wellbeing.*'

The Hallé also created community choirs for people in deprived areas of Manchester. The government gave special dispensation to perform Covid-compliant concerts and choral work because it was seen as vital care work for communities.

'*All these communities came together to sing and seeing each other in person again was incredibly emotional. It made a real difference. Prescribing patients with a range of ailments to work in music has been a huge growth area for health and social care generally in this country and is something that's definitely growing now.*

'While this work hasn't brought more funding from the Arts Council, it enabled us to provide them with evidence of the difference we're making with people suffering with dementia and particularly with young people, starting them on their musical journey.'

Putting people first, thinking flexibly and reaching out to collaborate and connect, not only helped the community but transformed its business. A great example of the Flexible Method in action.

We've seen how collaboration can take many different forms, ranging from simply networking with other businesses in the same sector and informally sharing information, problems or experiences to a formal alliance to work together on a project.

Particularly in a crisis, businesses can be stronger together and can seize opportunities or meet challenges they couldn't on their own.

The process of the Flexible Method requires a constant willingness to keep an open mind, listen and learn. It requires change. You will need to be adaptable as events unfold – there will be victory for the brave.

Adapt must be one of your watchwords. In the next chapter we focus in detail on this crucial skill.

The Flexible Method tools – Collaborate, connect

▶ Counter your instinct to hunker down – look outside for allies
▶ Reach out to your peers
▶ Lobby your industry and government with a stronger voice
▶ Embed collaboration in your culture
▶ Connect with your community through corporate citizenship

CHAPTER TEN

Adapt

The Masked Singer

The main spotlights fired up on the roof of the vast Bovingdon Studios, north of London. Executive producer Derek McLean gave a thumbs-up to the host, Joel Dommett, on stage. Nearby, the celebrity panelists, Davina McCall, Jonathan Ross, Rita Ora and Mo Gilligan, were sitting apart, separated by Perspex screens.

Instead of the roaring cheers from a studio audience of 300, there was only the clang of a distant door closing on the eerily empty set. The only people they would see were a few camera crew peering out from behind surgical masks.

Derek tried not to let his worry show:

'One of the key elements of a large-scale entertainment studio show is always the audience. Viewers at home probably don't real-ize that the atmosphere they're enjoying is created in the studio by the hundreds of people who are here to enjoy a live experience.

'During the pandemic this wasn't going to be possible, so having to come and perform in the middle of this huge studio without an audience was really nerve-wracking. And we really didn't know how this was going to come across because performers are used to

performing at a certain level and volume because they're project-
ing to an audience. It's a completely different experience to pro-
jecting to a silent room. You talk in a different way, your energy's
at a different level when an audience isn't there. We were really
conscious that the impact and atmosphere of the show could really
be affected.

'It was really hard for the panel and performers to get the meas-
ure of their performance when they were doing it in an empty
studio. It's a completely different thing for the four panelists who
are there to be funny and to react in a lively way, so they worked
with each other and became their own audience, laughing loudly
at jokes, responding positively to each other. In many ways, what
we saw was a friendlier and warmer atmosphere because people
were more generous and helping each other out. They were trying
to emulate what was absent.'

Davina McCall remembers proudly:

'It was actually one of the best shows we did. We all had to work
together and come up with solutions for this impossible task. It
created a greater sense of the team working together and when
we came to the filming days, there was such a buzz on set that we
were actually pulling this off. There was a crackle and energy in
the room that energized us all.'

The fact that we were able to shoot this crazy Saturday night
entertainment show for ITV at all during the pandemic was a
triumph of adaptation.

When Covid closed down all production we faced a daunting
task. How could we persuade the agents of A-list celebrities, let
alone the celebs themselves, to come into a closed environment,
put on costumes created by a team of strangers and then walk out
onto stage and perform a series of songs in public?

The key was to devise and implement a raft of Covid measures and a closed set. This had never been done before, but the whole team rose to the challenge. Anything less was just not an option.

Behind the mask

Normally we would have about 500 people working on the show, but how could they do their jobs if they couldn't work closely together?

Derek gives some context:

'One detail to give you context. One of the biggest issues in our industry during Covid was that makeup artists were a vector in transmitting the virus. And so we didn't know whether our stars of the show would be allowed to wear makeup.

'The idea of telling a celebrity that they might not be wearing makeup on television might seem like a trivial thing, but it can be career defining for that person. You can imagine the public have seen our talents in a certain way. For 10 years, 20 years, they've never been without makeup on television. So we didn't know if we were now going to have 40 individual makeup artists for each person, or would they have to do their own makeup?

'Some of the stars decided to bubble with their makeup artist and hairdresser or were very lucky because they were married to them. Others learned to do their own makeup. Everyone just became flexible and did what they could.'

We don't have to appear in front of an audience of millions every week, but do you remember feeling self-conscious about having to undergo your own personal close-up on Zoom with your lock-down hair? With the salons and barbers closed for months during Covid, millions of people were struggling with this issue.

I'm really proud of the way these teams adapted and ensured 'the show must go on'. Not only did they keep us in business; we got our staff back to work and were able to bring large numbers of freelancers back as well. I think they also cheered people up at a difficult time. It was win–win. The Flexible Method in action.

As an indie, Argonon is used to having to pivot in a rapidly changing marketplace. Bigger entities like the BBC are less nimble. Changes have to go through a lot of people in legal and business affairs and can be hard work – as we found during Covid.

Worzel Gummidge

This BBC scripted series starring, written and directed by Mackenzie Crook was put on hold by the pandemic. It is a family show about a magical scarecrow who comes to life and befriends two foster kids. The BBC told us there would be no drama filming *at all* in 2020 as it would be too tough and too risky to shoot. Crews were being laid off left, right and centre and companies were saddled with vast amounts of debt.

I knew that we had to get out to film *Worzel*. We needed to get back to work, help our top talent Mackenzie in every possible way, create employment for freelancers who were floundering with no furlough or help from the government. We just did not have the option to sit on our hands for a year.

Our team set about creating the most detailed Covid protocols imaginable to sanitize sets and keep crews socially distanced. The level of detail was eye-watering, from removing dressing room door handles to daily testing, closed catering and people living on set in separate bubbles.

It was going to be expensive but after weeks of cajoling and reassuring, the BBC agreed to help us fund the extra cost. We had created a gold standard set of practices which would be widely adopted across the industry. Because of this we were one of the first production companies to resume filming scripted drama in summer 2020.

Kristian Smith is the Executive Producer on *Worzel Gummidge*:

'I had to do quite a lot of soul-searching, signing off every single risk assessment. I was never going to do anything that I felt would wilfully endanger anybody. I understand the nervousness of the BBC, who commissioned Worzel Gummidge. *There were lots of meetings where we were asked questions. We really had to jump through a lot of fiery hoops.*

'Obviously, they were nervous times, but I did feel confident by the time we got to it that we were very prepared.'

The cast and crew used a system of concentric circles with people wearing colour-coded lanyards to see which bubble they were in. This reduced the risk of transmission, with everybody testing every day.

The cast included Vanessa Redgrave. Covid rules meant people over a certain age needed additional protections, so she came with her own helper, assistant and driver and they were a bubble. She had her own trailer, as did Mackenzie.

Normally on film sets, everyone's very convivial. There is lots of bustling activity, with people running around and eating together. This film set was very different.

Kristian details the procedure:

'There was 100 per cent mask wearing. It was a peculiar experience because film sets are really social. The policy was, you have your mask on the entire time unless you're having a drink or you're eating, and then you faced away from somebody else. It was really difficult for the more physical jobs, like prop moving, moving

lights, a lot of these people hadn't done their job with that kind of restriction.

'It was a really well-run operation with a zero-tolerance culture from the top down. It was the only way to protect everybody. We had put a clause in everybody's contract so that we could just remove them if they didn't abide by our Covid rules because it could have been life or death not to.

'And yet when the camera starts turning, the performers have to produce warmth and normality and humanity and their best work. One of the hardest things was saying, as soon as someone finished their take, you've got to go and stand outside on your own. And it's really hard because you can't go and have friendly chats, like you would want to as a producer. You could do it from a distance, but you could have no kind of intimacy. It was a real testament to each and every one of those actors, who had to turn up and just do it. And they did do it. They were great.'

We didn't have a single case of Covid on our shoot for *Worzel Gummidge*. I think the key to this success story was the can-do attitude of the management team and the way it enabled them to find a way around a seemingly insoluble problem. They put people first, gathered their generals to the Covid protocols, adapted and pushed through their decision with great commitment.

In other words, they used the Flexible Method.

It also helped that, unlike *The Masked Singer*, it was shot on outdoor locations during the summer.

Result

This ability to adapt is key to our success, and during crises to our very survival. It enabled our company to have a relatively decent turnover in 2020. Whereas the average hit on revenue taken by independent producers in 2020 was 19 per cent, ours was less than half of that, at 9 per cent. One of our biggest competitors took a whopping 30 per cent hit.

This illustrates how businesses must be adaptable, especially in a crisis. This means making swift, independent-minded decisions – a process that can become more turgid in bigger corporations. In some cases this can lead to the business going under.

Cutting remarks

Adapting doesn't always go smoothly, as celebrity hair stylist Michael Douglas discovered. He has styled everyone from Johnny Depp to Kate Moss and lives with TV host Davina McCall, which meant she was one of the lucky stars who lived with her hairdresser during Covid.

During lockdown Michael saw an enormous opportunity to connect with people and offer genuine help. He didn't realize that, of course, actions have consequences and not everybody agreed with his actions.

'There were hundreds of thousands of people out there who wanted help and advice about their hair and there wasn't a single hairdresser that I could see that was offering any. I think a lot of people felt really let down by their hairdresser. They were all basically saying to clients, "Don't touch your hair. Don't colour it, wait for the salons to open", which is contradictory to everything they'd said in the past, which was, "Oh, you should always get your hair done. You should always look nice. It's important to your mental health."

'I decided to go on Instagram Live for half an hour a day every day at 11:00 and just answer people's questions for them. People

can come on, ask me any question they like about their hair and I'll answer it. "What's the best shampoo for dry hair?" "What can I do if I've got highlights?" "What should I do if my roots are growing through?" All that kind of stuff.

'It became a really joyful thing. Everybody seemed to love it. Well, certainly everyone I was speaking to.

'I don't know if you've seen Instagram Live, but you get these questions that bump up at the bottom. And about every six questions or so, there would be a hairdresser basically abusing me and saying that I wasn't to be trusted, I wasn't a credible voice in the industry, I didn't know what I was talking about. And these were big, big names in the industry. They then got in touch with all my clients. They were absolutely taking me down and trying to ruin my entire reputation.'

Michael lost a couple of long-standing contracts with prime-time TV shows.

'I even got death threats. It just got very, very nasty, very quickly. Every time I opened my phone, there was just abuse of the worst kind. It was a classic case of being cancelled. I felt like JK Rowling for a bit. I was really terrified that my career was over. It was absolutely horrendous.

'In retrospect, I'd slightly misread the mood of the industry out there. I think hairdressers always thought that their businesses were future proof, that you will never get a robot to cut somebody's hair, so automation or computers aren't going to take over. And then out of nowhere, they all get shut down. I don't think anybody could believe it. I think the last thing they needed was somebody saying, "Don't worry about the hairdressers being closed, you can do your own hair." So it was badly worded by me, but the reaction was terrifying.

'The fear the hairdressing industry had was if you taught people how to do their hair at home, they wouldn't come back to the salon,

but I found it was the opposite. If you help people, they'll reward you with some loyalty. They'll come to your business and thank you for what you did for them during lockdown. Because in the end, people don't want to colour their own hair. They don't want to cut their own hair. They want to pay somebody to be responsible for it. And that hasn't changed at all. Virtually everyone I helped wanted to come and see me after for an appointment.'

Despite the backlash, Michael continued with his online hair advice concept and raised £2 million to launch a new business called Your Hair Anywhere, showing you how to style your hair anywhere in under ten minutes.

'I would say that at the moment my career is probably the best it's ever been and it's as a direct result of what happened to me. It was all good in the end. But bloody hell, it was painful.'

Using key elements of the Flexible Method, Michael put people first, communicated, adapted and pursued his idea with radical determination. One thing to be aware of, however, is that adopting this radical thinking will not always be well received by all your stakeholders. Actions always have consequences and it is worth considering what they will be and even sometimes moderating your actions as the situation demands. I'm glad that Michael's idea worked out well for him in the end.

Adaptable mindset

The Covid-19 pandemic saw businesses adapt to an astonishing extent, showing us what can be achieved with the right mindset. Some manufacturers switched to producing medical ventilators.

During lockdown, restaurants switched to home deliveries, gyms started online personal training, distillers repurposed to produce hand sanitizer, the electronics giant Sharp adapted a TV factory to make surgical masks. We saw human ingenuity everywhere we looked. It was remarkable and heart-warming.

Have you ever had to dramatically adapt to survive a crisis? How did it change your organization? What improvements has it brought about?

A crisis sometimes just accelerates a development you would probably have got around to eventually, such as the use of technology. Most of us had to switch to working remotely, using video technologies like Teams and Zoom.

Millennials are exemplary at adapting. It is in the DNA, having been born in an age of massive daily transformation as digital technology accelerates change. Millennials demonstrate flexible thinking and a willingness to try new things. If one thing becomes obsolete, just jump to the next, and back again if needs must.

As a result, many have now developed what I call a portfolio life. Georgia Maguire in London is an example. She is an actor, a stand-up comic, a comedy writer, a podcaster, an audiobook narrator and a chocolate maker. Oh, and she is also a wife and mother.

Or Harry Maguire, Georgia's brother, in Ho Chi Minh City, Vietnam. In addition to setting up a home in Asia, he is a management accountant, award-winning internet salesman, school administrator, foreign language teacher, part-time crypto investor and mountaineer.

These guys keep those plates spinning. It is a way of life. A multi-layered career keeps you fresh and stimulated as you deal with one challenge after another.

I'm sure you know plenty of examples in your own life. And perhaps you can also remember when you asked someone 'And what do you do?' and got a relatively straightforward answer. That's becoming a thing of the past!

As the leader of a team or an organization, you have no option about whether to change the way you do things, especially during a crisis which can transform your customer base overnight – how they communicate, their pain points, their accessibility. If you don't adapt, you may find you are suddenly irrelevant to them.

If your businesses is to survive and thrive, being an open-minded leader who can quickly adapt to change is crucial. Not only that, you must inspire your team to do the same.

On a positive note, you may find that a crisis forces your team to think more creatively and create different solutions. The changes you are forced to adopt may be beneficial in the long term, reducing your overheads and identifying new market opportunities.

Establishing a nimble and open-minded mindset in your team will enable you to be flexible enough to change direction if necessary and come out on top.

In fact, you need to act like a start-up. This will help you thrive in changed times. And let's face it, dramatic shifts are now happening so quickly that we have to adapt constantly as new opportunities arise or the external context renders your tried-and-tested ways of doing things obsolete.

Coast-to-coast creativity

I hired Lindsay Schwartz as Chief Creative Officer of Leopard USA during Covid, not just for her talent and experience but also because of her admirable adaptability.

When I first spoke to her, she was salvaging her slate of TV projects after the company she worked for had folded. Not only had she seen ten years' work threatened by the company going under, but Covid meant now she would have to manage a new team primarily based in New York via Zoom from Los Angeles – while working with a company headquartered in London.

A less adaptable person might have found this an insurmountable challenge, but it didn't faze Lindsay.

'I've always worked with people all over the world in previous jobs. I had already been through so much change that Covid didn't feel too different from what I had already gone through – the unknown. It was just more of the unknown.'

Lindsay began her career as an attorney in Beverly Hills, California, but realized that this career path was not for her. She made a decision that changed her entire life and followed her passion, starting over in a junior position as an executive assistant at a production company.

'I'm not a person who necessarily likes change. There are people that say, "Oh my gosh, I love change, it invigorates me." I'm not that way and that's evidenced by being at a company for ten years. But I am very flexible. It's a learned trait. I think everyone can learn to be flexible.'

Lindsay has been successful thanks to her flexible outside-the-box thinking. We always try to foster this at Argonon, but the pandemic forced us to step this up to another level, using the Flexible Method to put people first, communicate and adapt.

Being open to new ways of working is now part of our everyday, but some crises change the marketplace so fundamentally that adapting your operations is no longer enough: you will have to come up with an entirely new business model.

This will demand that you supercharge your creativity, a challenging but positive process that we turn to now.

The Flexible Method tools – Adapt

▶ Establish a nimble and open-minded mindset

▶ Be open to new ways of working

▶ Be prepared that some people may not like your new adaptation

▶ Be flexible, evolving as the situation evolves

CHAPTER ELEVEN

Supercharge your creativity

Smart move

The preschoolers at the Kids R Us Learning Center in Brookhaven, Mississippi, were particularly lively this Monday morning as La'Ron Hines started work. A boy and girl were squealing excitedly over a colouring book while another four-year-old was quietly banging a drum in the corner.

La'Ron, 19, sighed and reached for a tissue. It felt a long way from Hollywood where he had just been trying to get a break as an actor, singer and dancer. Then Covid hit. His classes closed and the auditions dried up. He had to move back in with his parents in Mississippi and work at their daycare centre.

'It felt like my career was at a standstill. I knew what I wanted to do: I wanted to be in the entertainment industry. My mom was telling me, I can't just sit in the house all day, just because the world is on lockdown doesn't mean I have to be on lockdown. So I started to help out with the kids.'

Instead of regarding the setback to his career as a drudge or a bore, La'Ron asked himself: How can I turn this particular unique set of circumstances to my advantage? How can I adapt? He saw an opportunity and seized the day.

'It was just all a matter of me finding time within myself to be creative.'

Talking to the kids, he realized how funny they were. He filmed them answering some simple questions and with their parents' consent posted the video on TikTok.

'It was an instant hit. People were loving the content that I was putting out. It got millions of views, so I was just very excited for that.

'I started thinking, I can use this to my advantage, where it's fun for everybody. The kids can have fun, I can have fun. It keeps them occupied and having a good time.

'I tried to turn something that was seen as a negative into a positive. We started to do more of the videos.'

He called the TikTok series 'Are You Smarter than a Preschooler?' He made more than 130 episodes and it attracted the attention of celebrities such as singers Robin Thicke and Beyoncé, and comedians Tina Fey and Amy Poehler, who invited him to appear at the Golden Globes.

Lindsay Schwartz, Chief Creative Officer at Leopard USA, takes up the story:

'La'Ron was a great TikTok talent, doing these incredible, really funny segments – adorable videos with all these kids from his mom's daycare, asking them questions, and they would have the silliest answers. Or doing dances with them or singing with them. So that's the really heartfelt, sweet content that absolutely blew up.

'Then we thought, what would a show with him be like? And so we dove into his world and all of the amazing things happening

around him. And we were really interested in this kind of duality of his life where he has one foot in Mississippi and he's helping his parents, who are the salt of the earth, with his mom's daycare and his dad's ice-cream truck and bounce-house business, versus his relationship with Robin Thicke and him building his career out in LA.

'He's incredibly talented. He could be the next Justin Bieber. So we put together the tape and it garnered the attention of Snapchat.'

La'Ron and Leopard USA have now been commissioned to produce this series for Snapchat. La'Ron says:

'Without the pandemic, I don't know what I would've been doing. I would've still been trying to pursue my music and acting, but I would not have seen as much success from it as I've seen with the social media. In 2020, I was like, "Man, I wish the world was opening up." But I feel like it was a blessing in disguise.'

I love his story. La'Ron could have thrown in the towel after his Hollywood dreams were crushed by Covid. Instead, he supercharged his creativity to find a golden opportunity in the less promising surroundings of his mum's daycare centre.

His experience echoes our own at Argonon. The pandemic brought us opportunities we never would have had or might have had to wait years for.

People who used the Flexible Method to seize opportunities and demonstrate that even when times are tough, they can really pull imaginative, good work out of the box, have really benefited. The pandemic has brought a lot of talent to the fore that maybe wouldn't have come through so quickly. So while it has been very tough – I've got my own war wounds, we all have – it has given us amazing opportunities.

You must adapt your business in a crisis, and often more than just a tweak is required – you may have to create whole new ways of working and a new set of clients.

While on the subject of creativity, I don't believe people should be divided into creative and non-creative. We all have the ability to innovate, think and experiment. You just need the confidence to do it.

Changing spots

When the Credit Crunch hit the TV industry hard, producer David Chikwe was working for Leopard Pictures, an independent scripted production company within the Argonon group.

'Watching the news and seeing people walking out of their offices with those classic cardboard boxes, I thought, is that going to be me? I've just bought my first home and now the economy's gone down the toilet. How am I going to be able to keep my head above water?

'Thinking logically, one area that was less affected by the crisis was the BBC, which didn't have the same financial pressures as the commercial networks. I already had a relationship with a BBC commissioner, Damien Kavanaugh, who had moved from Daytime to Children's at CBBC.

'Children's was a new genre for us, but I had always loved children's TV. I spent pretty much my entire childhood having my mum telling me to stop watching TV from when I'd come home at 4 o'clock in the afternoon.'

Despite David's love of the genre, making children's programming our new focus was a big punt as Leopard was a very small team and it took a lot of confidence to commit all of his time to this. It was risky, but we decided to go for it.

David developed a slate of three children's ideas. This was quite an investment for the company. And then all of the ideas were rejected. It was a blow. We regrouped. We decided to soldier on, committed to cracking this new client. David continues:

'I had held back one idea: it was about a robot called Eve who gets adopted by a human family and has to figure out how to be a real girl. The idea was ET meets Pinocchio. When I pitched this, the commissioner's eyes sparkled!'

This ultimately led to a commission for 36 episodes and was absolutely transformative for Leopard and for David's career. He developed and co-created the series. By series three, he was overall series producer. *Eve* won a clutch of awards and later David went on to write his own original scripts and then set up his own production company, something he had never even considered before.

So instead of destroying his career, the Credit Crunch opened a door for him.

'You have to be in the moment and live for now and not be afraid to take risks when these opportunities are presented to you. These usually turn out to be the best moments of your career because you're forced to think about things differently. The crisis was definitely one of those moments when I thought, yes, I can originate ideas myself. Yes, I can get things commissioned and make my own opportunities with the fullest creative ownership.

'Life experiences had taught me that if you think clearly, if you push ahead, if you take some calculated risks, then you're probably going to find a way through.'

David illustrates all the key points for supercharging your creativity: fearlessly taking risks, collaborating, then resolutely advancing the idea to a positive result.

I'm sure his story will resonate with moments in your own life when you were able to seize opportunities that arose from disasters.

House Hunters International

We produce a series in the US called *House Hunters International*, which is a real estate series on HGTV and Discovery+. It follows people who are moving to exotic locations and need a new home to live in. We film the series 365 days a year on all continents.

When all filming got shut down in March 2020, the travel industry was also thrown into chaos. This was something we had not prepared for. Like many production companies, we could have shut up shop for the duration, but the series is a major employer of staff, both permanent and freelance, and an important part of our turnover.

So we got together and examined whether there was a way to resume shooting *House Hunters International* despite the travel bans. If we couldn't fly out crew from New York and London, could we outsource the filming locally?

We had never done this on such a scale before and there was some anxiety about the idea of working with local film crews around the world rather than our own people. Some colleagues distrusted the expertise of a local crew: *'they just don't have the same skills.'* Well, this may have been true sometimes, but now we had no option.

We set Covid protocols in place, got sign-off from Discovery, our main producing partner, to shoot and by June we were back filming. We recruited brilliantly talented producers, directors and camera operators all over the world, particularly in places where Covid lockdowns were lifting: Egypt, Finland, Majorca, Guatemala and Mexico. We trained them meticulously and set them to work.

The next thing we did was seek to mine our assets. We dug into our archive and produced a 'Where are they now?' spinoff series following contributors from previous episodes. We thought our audience would like to hear their stories about how they had gone on to fulfil more of their dreams since the original episode had aired.

We also pushed the envelope creatively, shooting new drone and action sequences to really update the feel of the series. We called it *The Adventure Continues.*

One major challenge was that the series director, Liz Layton, was pregnant, so we had to keep her safe from the pandemic. She had to learn how to direct the series remotely in 12 countries around the world from her apartment on the East Coast of the US, shooting action sequences using drones via WhatsApp, FaceTime and Zoom. The entire series was edited from home from around the tri-state area in New York.

When the first edit arrived in my inbox, I have to admit I was trepidatious. What if the material looked or felt less than super high-end? We pride ourselves on excellent production values. Nothing less will do.

I opened the link in my inbox and watched. The film started with an incredible series of drone sequences and then action shots, then a very warm and engaging interview with a couple who were making a huge success of their new life in Australia. I need not have worried: the team had pulled off an amazing feat. This was the start of something new!

The results exceeded our expectations. In fact, it has been so successful that we are not going back to the old way of doing things. We have become bigger and stronger as a team and will not look back. We also saved a considerable amount of money on flights and hotel accommodation, not to mention no jet lag and fewer carbon emissions.

This was another win thanks to the Flexible Method: putting people first, collaborating and above all supercharging our creativity.

Had we thought about this earlier and been better prepared, we might have implemented these changes sooner.

Has a crisis ever forced you to innovate and boost your creativity? If so, can you break down the process into replicable steps?

Gutted

During the pandemic, many businesses I know had to transform themselves to win new markets. They came up with ideas, some big and some small, and pursued them fearlessly.

At the Birmingham Hippodrome, CEO Fiona Allan was faced with what seemed an insoluble crisis. Even though theatres were allowed to reopen in the summer of 2020 with social distancing, the required 50 per cent reduction in the audience meant it was uneconomical to run, as staffing and operational costs would have remained exactly the same. She says: *'It was actually a lot cheaper for us to keep the technical bits of the theatre decommissioned for the period. Stop-starting is really expensive.'*

Then Fiona came up with a brainwave. It was a radical move that required total commitment. How about stripping all the seats out of the venue and turning it into a giant, socially distanced exhibition space?

She looked at 'Van Gogh Alive', a multi-sensory immersive experience, projecting massive images of the artist's work onto walls. Perhaps that could work in the Hippodrome using the stalls and stage area as a backdrop? She took the plunge and licensed the exhibition. They gutted the entire theatre of seats to create a space where visitors could stay socially distanced. A system of timed entry would also stagger the number of people in any part of the building at any one time.

'The benefits were multiple: besides bringing in revenue it gave the team something really positive to focus on after spending months refunding tickets, seeing some of their peers made redundant or being on furlough. It also allowed us to bring 100 to 150 of our freelance workforce back.

'It was the only cultural offering going on in the city all day, every day and the response was amazing. People just needed to go and do something cultural. It was almost cathartic. We had people in tears, just saying they had missed being with other people and having a live cultural experience.'

Fiona used key elements of the Flexible Method – thinking flexibly, putting people first, supercharging her creativity and then following this through with fierce resolve. Her actions saved the venue and greatly boosted its standing with its stakeholders.

Would you and your team have the courage and creativity to change your business so radically if required? If not, I'd like to offer some tips that we have derived from crises over the years.

First off, don't try to be perfect. In a crisis, when innovation is a matter of survival, don't worry about perfection when you're innovating – just try something new, put it out there, adapting as you learn and grow.

Take imperfect action. Creativity is often a messy, iterative process – just take a look at the footage of The Beatles recording together in the documentary *Get Back* on Disney+.

Don't be scared of bad ideas either. In my experience, people who don't have bad ideas don't come up with any good ones either. In fact, not changing and clinging to routine are much more worrying for me than change. Change is good.

When you do go for it, you have to overcome self-doubt, trust in your abilities and have the passion, hunger and drive to make it happen.

Creative block? Try changing your workplace. Go to a café or a park. A new environment really can help your brain to think differently.

Still stuck for fresh ideas? Take a break and do nothing. Leave your to-do list behind and clear your head. Sleep and rest help you generate good ideas. Your mind is more innovative when you are free of the noise and clutter of routine. You will be more inspired when you return refreshed.

And to survive a crisis long enough to turn creativity into cash, you're also going to need all the help you can get. You may be surprised, but if you seek help, you will probably find it out in the real world in abundance. In the next chapter I'll share with you how we and other business leaders successfully sought help in a crisis.

The Flexible Method tools – Supercharge your creativity

▶ Embrace risk – not changing can be more risky
▶ Be bold in your creativity
▶ Overcome self-doubt, trust your abilities
▶ Pursue your ideas with radical commitment

CHAPTER TWELVE

Seek help

Orchestral manoeuvres

The conductor raised his hands to indicate that the piece was to begin. The delicate notes of the oboe floated from his laptop speakers. But as soon as the strings came in, he waved his hands: *'No, no, no! Stop!'* He had never heard such awful discordance from the Hallé Orchestra. They were playing out of time!

Performing an online concert had seemed a great idea. Indeed, it was their only option with live music venues closed by the Covid-19 pandemic. Without income from performances, the orchestra would not survive. But getting 40 musicians to play seamlessly together on Zoom from their own homes was impossibly complicated, particularly as a slight lag meant they heard notes a couple of seconds after they were played.

David Butcher, Chief Executive, the Hallé Concerts Society, and his team thought about where they could get help. *'It was clear that we needed to massively step up our IT capabilities. We already worked with some pretty big companies like Siemens through corporate choirs. They have good IT departments so we asked if they could help.'*

Keen to continue their weekly sessions with the Hallé's choral conductors for their staff, companies helped fund new equipment. *'We were also lucky to get a six-figure grant from the Garfield Weston Foundation who loved what we were doing and felt the Hallé was being innovative.'*

Their digital department of two was expanded to four people. They learned to mix the sound from individual voices and instruments so they could actually hear the full choir when they were singing. They also invested in professional lighting and camera equipment to film the orchestra's performances.

David considers what they have learned from the experience:

'It was a huge learning curve for us. We've also been asking the players to work in different ways so they've become very adaptable. Whether it's been through digital means, doing a one-to-one masterclass with a student by Zoom, or filming a concert. They've been challenged by it and I think they've embraced it.

'It gives much greater accessibility. We can reach people on the other side of the world or people with disabilities or people that can't leave home, or people who just can't travel that day. It's opened up the world for us.'

The Hallé's filmed performances online now bring about 20 per cent of their income from abroad as the brand has expanded.

'It's been revolutionary in terms of changing what we might do, but I think it's given us a bit more licence to be braver in terms of programming. So with the films we commissioned two or three different people to write new music. And new music is the lifeblood for us going forward.'

Faced with an existential crisis, the orchestra used elements of the Flexible Method – collaborating, connecting, supercharging their creativity, seeking help and then following it through with great resolve –to transform its business .

Reach out

In a crisis, it is a positive strength to reach out for help rather than stubbornly struggle alone. It demonstrates that you are a realist and a pragmatist. Both of these positions are core tools of the Flexible Method.

Do not resist asking for help for yourself and your business.

It is a widely held belief that people, more often than not men, should always stand strong and never show vulnerability. I grew up in a family where my parents acted on that assumption – and told me that showing vulnerability was evidence that you were oversensitive, somehow deficient.

That is unhelpful and I have spent time in adult life unpicking that belief.

For me, vulnerability is strength and part of the whole. All humans are made up of layers. We have multiple facets, we have huge potential to do great things, we all get depressed sometimes. This is what it means to be human. And to acknowledge and own this rich tapestry of experience is to be truly a rounded human being. It also makes for a wiser and more resilient leader.

Vulnerability goes hand in hand with sensitivity. And sensitivity, I have learned, is one of my core strengths. My job is to devise ideas and then produce them with talented, creative people. We have to dig deep to make our programmes resonate. We make a good living from tapping into and revealing our sensitive side and we speak to millions of people all over the world through our shows.

Sensitivity also makes me a better leader. Sensitivity and emotional intelligence go hand in hand. I regard emotional intelligence as another of my core strengths. It empowers me to work closely with creative people in a highly strung industry where the stakes can be high.

So, whatever your industry or field is, I ask you to allow yourself to be everything that you are and not to resist the whole range of good and bad that make up our lives. Increasingly, young people coming into the workforce demand authenticity from their leaders – so be real. Be yourself.

Fighting not failing

During the Covid-19 pandemic, governments around the world offered financial support to keep the economy alive. The US federal government offered unprecedented levels of loans and tax credits to incentivize companies not to lay off workers. In the UK, employers could get a grant called furlough to cover up to 80 per cent of the wages for employees not working due to coronavirus restrictions.

The hospitality industry was hit particularly hard by lockdown, so I was shocked when my friend Ed Templeton said he hadn't applied for any state aid for his restaurant business. The reason? He felt too embarrassed to ask for help.

I understand this sentiment. Nobody likes to look needy, but I strongly encouraged him to rethink. He listened and acted. I am so glad I was able to be there for him. His business took government support and is doing well.

The conversation with Ed made me realize how uneasy some people are about asking for help in a crisis. Business owners are probably more independent-minded and reluctant to ask for support. It's hardwired in us to do things ourselves. The thought of surrendering control to someone else, especially an anonymous bureaucrat, is not easy.

The fear of being perceived as weak and needy is real. It is one of the reasons that drives people to become leaders in the first place – we can do this ourselves!

Nobody likes to admit they are failing either. I do understand – I went through these feelings myself when the pandemic threatened the survival of my business.

The truth is that asking for help does not mean you are failing. Quite the opposite. It means you are fighting!

This is another reason why it is helpful to have a diverse range of personality types in your leadership team. People will react differently to situations and as leader you can then make your decision based on a set of options.

Feisty fundraiser

Fortunately for us, Laura Bessell, Argonon COO, had no qualms about seeking help as she fought to keep our business afloat during lockdown. In fact, she had a downright feisty attitude towards it:

'We looked for every scheme that could possibly support us and became absolute experts at it. We went into so much detail that we made sure that everybody in the group that could be applicable for the scheme was included, and that did take a lot of work to be on the right side of the law.

'I found out about finance packages available in the US from networking with American business owners. Talking to peers and colleagues across the globe was really, really important in making us more aware of what packages were available for US-owned or US-based companies because it was a very different scheme from what was on offer in the UK, for example. That created a lot of liquidity for us.

'In the US, the money was loaned directly to the company. It was based on the number of people you had to lay off at the beginning of the pandemic and then how many people you were able to re-employ. And because we pushed really, really hard in the US to get back into production, we were only out of production for three months. Because we let a lot of people go and then brought a lot of people back after those three months, we were able to have what was called a forgiveness element of the loan, which wrote off the loans, and a lot of that cash went back into the company to reward it for rehiring all those people.

'I sit on the PACT finance committee, so I'm able to network with people on that side of things. PACT is our industry association which supports independent producers and is really good at leveraging the government. Insurance was difficult because until the government Restart scheme began in January 2021 it was really difficult to go into production on big productions. Leveraging PACT to get them to push the government was absolutely critical for this.'

Laura used key elements of the Flexible Method to reach out to peers on Zoom during lockdown to get information about aid schemes and collaborate with our industry association to lobby the government. Without this, we would not have been able to work during the pandemic.

Please, sir, may I have some more?

Not everyone has a financial expert in-house to cut through the red tape to get government loans, so smaller businesses may have to reach outside their organization for help – perhaps from a trade organization or more informal contacts.

I urge you to take whatever is on offer and then ask for more. Channel your inner Oliver Twist. It is the first responsibility of governments to keep their people alive and well and we must demand that they deliver on that.

While Ed was reluctant to put out his hand for state aid during the pandemic, he did reach out for help in relation to his young team's employment rights and welfare. He contacted an industry peer, who is head of HR for a restaurant group.

'She was an unbelievable resource throughout the whole thing. She talked about mental health within hospitality and also looking after your people and your team. And made a point of constantly feeding us information that she was getting and sharing. They have a team of lawyers and all sorts of people and resources that we didn't necessarily have access to.

'She spent time with me on the phone, things like redundancies, which we'd never had to face before. How does that work? What does it look like? How do you do it obviously in the nicest way possible... and try to find the least bad solution for the people who you're speaking to? But also ensuring that from a legal and HR perspective, you're not getting yourself into any hot water.

'She was amazing. Luckily a lot of the part-time staff qualified for the furlough scheme. We made sure that everybody who could get access to it did.'

Call your clients

John and Rob Grim had mixed fortunes when they reached out for help when the pandemic closed their chain of gyms. To stay in business, they first sought help from their clients, asking if they would commit to buying online PT sessions and paying in advance.

John outlines his approach: *'I just basically went through all the top spenders and I took a couple of afternoons out and rang up, cap in hand, and said, look, we need your help.'*

Rob chips in: *'You were honest. You didn't sugarcoat and say, oh I can do you a deal or some nonsense like that. It was like, look, we're a small business, we're a family business and we need your help. And our clients were amazing.'*

John recalls: *'In a couple of afternoons, I secured a large sum of upfront payments that we then had to service.'* That was a life saver, says Rob.

The brothers were less successful in renegotiating their rents. They got three half-price months from their landlords, but as they were locked down for ten months this still meant severe cuts on expenditure and belt-tightening to survive.

Artistic licence

At the Birmingham Hippodrome, CEO Fiona Allan managed to secure government help during the pandemic:

'It was very difficult for us as an independent charity organiza-tion trying to argue for culture recovery funding. We don't normally go asking the Arts Council for money and we did join forces with about ten other independent organizations like us across muse-ums and galleries and theatres to lobby government. We applied for the full three million and we got it without argument for the Hippodrome. What we were strongly saying was, we won't ask for help again but if you help us stabilize now we will go back to being independent and not begging for money, but we need the interven-tion now in order for that to happen. It just took us a little while but they did get that messaging.'

Sometimes it is the state that asks for help from business. During Covid-19, the New York City Economic Development Corporation called for emergency medical supplies and 1,700 local companies responded to manufacture the likes of face shields and ventilators, with Century 21 stores donating trucks for transport.

If there was one good thing to come out of that whole awful time it was the way people stepped up and responded to calls from help in every direction. I'm sure you played your part, but ask yourself: did you get all the help you needed?

When the next crisis hits, do make sure you reach out and get all the help you can instead of trying to cope alone. After all, you have a duty to look after your organization and team when they are under terrible strain, a subject we turn to next.

The Flexible Method tools – Seek help

▶ Asking for help is a sign of strength, not weakness
▶ Reach out to your stakeholders – and help them in return
▶ Also seek all the non-financial help that is available

CHAPTER THIRTEEN

Care for your team's mental health

It was like living in the movie *28 Days Later*. The normally bustling streets of London were eerily empty as I ventured out for supplies. A lady approached clutching her scarf to her face, then stepped off the pavement to avoid me, her eyes full of mistrust, fearful of even breathing close to another soul.

I was wearing gloves and a mask too, thinking the whole world was contaminated during those early days of Covid-19. Going outside was pretty depressing, but at home and work I was also surrounded by people suffering from extreme anxiety. One colleague went into complete meltdown, stocking up on baked beans and saying he was never going to leave the house again.

We had a flood at the office in the middle of lockdown and no plumber dared to venture out to fix it. Our cleaners were also frightened to go into the offices and set up a system where the whole place was sanitized every single time anyone went in to collect a piece of equipment. This was time consuming and expensive, so for three months we basically stopped anyone entering or leaving any of our buildings.

I was extremely concerned about people at Argonon working from home with children. There was a sense of despair when we were told that schools were not going to be reopening and people couldn't come into the office. People were struggling with limited space at home, having to battle on with meetings while children played noisily in the background.

I was acutely aware of this and knew we had to grapple with it head on.

Did the pandemic also impact your team's mental health? What measures did you take to deal with this?

Endemic anxiety

These are worrying times, with pandemics, war, terrorism, economic, political and social unrest, and climate change. Throw in the daily stresses of family and work life and is it any surprise that people are so stressed and anxious?

Younger managers tend to be more affected than older people who have more experience to cope. A major crisis can leave your team suffering from shock, helplessness, worries about colleagues, fear about future incidents or guilt.

Years ago, the issue of employee mental health was regarded as something that was people's own business, something you wouldn't get involved in, but thankfully attitudes have changed.

Research shows that caring for mental health in the workplace is not a nice-to-have concept: it impacts your bottom line due to loss in productivity, or the cost of replacing staff who leave. It costs companies billions, so improving the management of mental health in the workplace, including prevention and early identification of problems, could save employers money.

Surveys show that one in six workers are likely to suffer from a mental health condition in any one year and that work-related stress accounts for around half of all working days lost due to ill health (Lelliott and Tulloch, 2008; HSE, 2021).

In a crisis you are going to need your whole team to pull out the stops to get through it. They are not going to be able to do this if they are impeded by mental health problems. So as a leader, caring for your team's mental health is a key task.

In my company, we are used to people getting sick sometimes and we do not judge or pigeon-hole them. Quite the opposite: we take physical and mental problems as part of life – difficult but unavoidable. We go out of our way to support our people and offer help wherever we can. Not only is this kindness and a vital human response to difficulty, it is also a reflection of the sort of company we are.

Barriers to mental health

While there is increasing awareness of the impacts of poor employee mental health, there is still a disconnect between employers' intentions and what is actually done in the workplace. There remains a stigma about mental health issues in some quarters and it is our job to change that. We make it clear to all our team that diversity and inclusion include invisible conditions and situations. But still fear exists.

A British national employee mental wellbeing survey found a third of employees did not approach anyone for support when they experienced poor mental health. Around half of people with mental health problems said they would not be comfortable talking to their employer (Cholteeva, 2022).

People have concerns about confidentiality and the impact on their career if they admit they are struggling. People are worried that if they speak up about feeling traumatized, others might think they are creating problems. They fear being seen as weak if they ask for help and so they try to act as if they are stronger and more resilient than they actually are. As a result, they tend to bottle up their feelings, sometimes to the point where those feelings become so intense they can't function any more.

I've already suggested that as leaders we may have a stronger impulse to hide weakness and struggle on in silence. But have you ever experienced someone in your team struggling and bottling up their emotions? When someone else is doing this, I think you can see the folly of it more clearly.

Have you ever allowed yourself to reveal your own difficulty if you are having a bad day at work? I admit that I have had to learn to do this. In my opinion it is important for us all to be able to reveal ourselves to our colleagues sometimes. Work is not a place to gush out all your problems, but it should be a safe place to be authentic, even if it means bursting into tears in a crisis. You may think that's a step too far, but let's cut each other some slack.

Another barrier is lack of knowledge and resources to address workforce mental health and wellbeing. Line managers are not trained psychiatrists. Nor should they be. It is a good idea though for your senior management team to have an understanding of mental health issues and have some training.

I would suggest you consider some of the following key actions:

▶ Put workplace mental health and wellbeing on the agenda.
▶ Establish a culture of proactive, preventative management of workplace wellbeing.
▶ Appoint a lead dedicated to mental wellbeing.
▶ Regularly survey your staff about their mental health.
▶ Monitor key performance indicators.

Resources

There are now many resources available to help staff, including 24/7 confidential support helplines and online therapy. Here's what a few companies offered during Covid:

▶ The retailer Target offered its US employees a year of access to Daylight, a website and app designed to help users navigate stress and worry, and Sleepio, an app that provides self-help tools to improve sleep. Target employees already had access to a company programme offering benefits including five free counselling sessions.

▶ The assurance, advisory and tax services company PwC offered employees access to wellbeing coaches and an online community to discuss mental health topics. The firm already offers employees and dependants six free therapy sessions and free apps on guided meditations, sleep, breathing and relaxing music.

▶ The software company Salesforce offered employees a series of articles and webinars on emotional health, as well as a meditation app, in addition to free face-to-face or video counselling sessions.

▶ The assurance, tax, transaction and advisory services company EY offers its employees 24/7 resources through its programme, which connects employees to healthcare professionals. During the pandemic it enhanced a suite of offerings around emotional wellbeing so employees could access free mobile apps for building emotional resilience and improving sleep habits.

▶ In addition to one-to-one counselling with clinicians, the company added daily group counselling sessions for parents and adult caregivers, a free 12-week course on mindfulness and daily scheduled practice sessions. EY also began daily drop-in sessions combining short mindfulness exercises with practical tips for managing anxiety, social isolation, feeling overwhelmed, etc. During Covid, EY's global chairman launched a recognition programme highlighting EY people doing exceptional things to support each another, their communities or clients.

▶ The energy company Chevron gives staff access to licensed counsellors to help employees cope with fear, anxiety and other emotions or concerns. It ran a corporate-wide mental health campaign to increase awareness and reduce stigma associated with mental health. Self-guided resilience resources are also accessible for all employees.

▶ The news organization the *Financial Times* provided regular one-on-one counselling and bespoke webinars for its employees on a variety of topics. Staff can already access meditation via the Headspace app, plus a weekly, virtual, guided meditation session. To counter the impact of reduced social connections on employees' mental wellbeing, they held regular video sessions to chat and share tips on topics like staying active and great podcasts. An annual mental health awareness week has workshops on topics like better sleep. They also offered animal therapy for employees and their families.

These examples show how proactive care is now mainstream and taken seriously by major companies.

At my company, where diversity and inclusion are always at the front of our minds, we also put a lot of actions into place. Working closely with our HR teams in London, New York and LA we introduced the following for all employees during the Covid pandemic:

- ▶ employee assistance programme with free, confidential counselling
- ▶ full sick pay if an employee was unable to work from home
- ▶ regular business town halls to stay connected through virtual working
- ▶ regular communications from senior management to all group companies
- ▶ regular communications from HR to all staff
- ▶ open (virtual) door policy from senior management to talk through staff concerns
- ▶ hybrid working to empathize with staff anxiety about return to office
- ▶ FAQ document with information on everything from tax issues to mental health
- ▶ trained mental health first aiders across the group
- ▶ annual departmental catch-ups with the CEO each holiday season. I found these particularly enjoyable as it was a chance to talk openly with each team about their year, the ups and the downs. It also provided me with invaluable feedback on changes that needed to be implemented
- ▶ an overhaul and update of family-friendly policies
- ▶ regular check-ins from head of HR to heads of business to ensure they had the right support tools for their staff.

Smaller employers may not have such a range of resources but will be better able to spot an employee who is struggling with mental health issues.

Psychological support in the workplace is often reactive rather than proactive. This is where strong interpersonal relationships at work become important sources of support, especially from managers.

Our line managers often sent little gifts to their teams during the pandemic – chocolates, flowers, drinks, etc. This made our teams feel valued. Their hard work was being noticed and appreciated.

Fun time!

Good general communication about the business situation is vital in a crisis, but sometimes it is good to just take time out and have some fun.

Spending time with colleagues and using humour are ways of distancing yourself from the horrors of a traumatic incident. The emergency services, army and journalists are renowned for the black humour they use to cope with what they have to deal with. My team and I had plenty of opportunities to share our predicament and we made sure we often laughed together.

Set up social activities that encourage your staff to socialize. This can involve after-work drinks, company trips and a buddy system for new hires. And if your team are working remotely, remember that they have little time to chat to each other, so use virtual meetings as opportunities for them to do this before you get down to business.

Asked what approach the company took, Shirley Escott, COO of Leopard USA, says:

'I hold weekly Teams meetings with casting/production and development to check in on productions as well as how the individual teams are.

'To try to keep a sense of community during Covid we held a remote Christmas party. All staff received a gift and we had "hangout" rooms with a quiz/music chat.'

At Argonon we had regular virtual coffees and chats. I also thoroughly enjoyed meeting my colleagues' children and pets online. My two cocker spaniels went down a treat in a couple of meetings. Just don't overdo it!

Ed Templeton noticed his staff were becoming mentally exhausted during the pandemic as his restaurant business was constantly reinventing itself and trying new things. His chefs were being asked to do a lot more, sometimes outside their comfort zone, with accelerated changes.

To improve morale, they ran blind wine-tasting sessions online. Ed says:

'Everyone was posted unlabelled bottles and we sat there on Zoom and our wine expert talked it through. We had sheets that she'd prepared that had a bit of a guessing game and explanation of the different wines. It's a kind of education in the sense that we're learning about the different wines, but it was just something that was not talking about how we're going to get through the next few months and what's going on in the business. It's just a nice way of everyone being together in a virtual space.

'We did skills shares with chefs as well – cooking recipes online like a masterclass workshop with everybody getting the ingredients.'

Pay attention and listen

Many larger companies have found that providing education and training about mental health in the workplace can be beneficial, encouraging supportive workplace relationships, reducing stigma and developing listening skills and empathy.

You don't need to be a big organization to foster a culture where people care and look out for colleagues. The advantage of this is that problems can be spotted in time. Concerned team members can tell when someone is not their usual self and recognize there may be a problem, for example increased irritability, lack of focus or being more quiet than usual.

I would encourage you to be empathetic and listen. Take the time to talk to employees, ask open questions, such as what help they need. We are probably all guilty of being a little too fond of the sound of our own voice at times, so make sure you listen without judging or interrupting. Let them disclose as much or as little as they feel comfortable doing. And this is not a one-off exercise. You should regularly follow up and reassess.

Appraisals can be useful for addressing drops in performance which may signal that a staff member might be experiencing distress.

Remember that change processes during a crisis can be especially anxious for staff who have a history of mental health problems. They may fear being made redundant and need extra support.

As a manager you need to take a more proactive approach to looking after the wellbeing of your staff. Pay attention to people you interact with, especially when using video communications, when it's harder to pick up cues. Regularly take the time to check in with your team and ask how they are doing. Even, or especially, if they are off sick.

Psychotherapist Emily Arikian is a team manager for an outpatient mental health clinic in New York City. During Covid she and her team had to adjust to providing counselling online during this anxious period, when many clients were alone at home. Emily says:

'So much of anxiety treatment is just refocusing on what you can control to help feel prepared and obviously build self-awareness around triggers to develop coping skills.

'Usually, we'd rate how much of a problem is it for me that I can't control this? If it's a ten, why is it a ten? Why isn't it a nine? So a lot of motivational interviewing, open-ended questions and then figuring out ways to navigate it.

'Sometimes just accepting that these things cannot be controlled and therefore there's nothing you can do and just let it happen. Live with it. I have to be okay with the fact that I'm not okay with this and there's nothing I can really do about it.

'One of the things that my boss put me in charge of was investing in our team's health. I would always allot a decent amount of time just to check in and ask a lot of open-ended questions. How are you doing? What's that like for you? What are some things that have come up that have not felt so good? How do you feel like you're doing? How would you rate your own performance? What can we do to help you feel more confident and stronger here?

'When you are not face to face you can hide things easier, such as if you have been drinking. When you can see them in person, most people suffering from problems will show some red flags.

'We also had monthly initiatives, from staff lunches to ice-cream parties, to just sending out appreciation emails when they do a good job, encouraging time off because in the American business system employees feel so guilty taking time off. It's not encouraged, but you're not going to give 100 per cent if you're not 100 per cent.'

I believe that a culture that values authenticity and openness will encourage staff to be their complete selves at work and share problems early on. Lindsay Schwartz, Chief Creative Officer of Leopard US, takes this approach:

'Our jobs, especially from home, get very intermingled into our personal life and our work never stops. I appreciate when my team come to me and they say, "You know what, everybody's really overwhelmed right now. Can we not do this this week?" And I say, "Absolutely."

I listen. I'm very cognizant of not wanting people to burn out. So we talk about what to do when people are getting to that point.

'*I think people's vacation days are very important. Everybody should be able to take them and take that time off because you come back, in the creative space, especially refreshed. Creatively, your ideas are your number one asset. If you're not able to have the space to come up with those incredible, fresh, creative ideas, then we're losing a lot from that employee. They need to be able to rejuvenate and refresh to be able to come back to have those ideas.*'

A supportive workplace atmosphere and close relationships with colleagues mean you can always talk to somebody honestly after a stressful day and feel you will be listened to. We cope with fear and feeling overwhelmed by crises when we feel supported and that we are part of a bigger, caring whole. This is a pillar of the Flexible Method.

How does your organization compare? Is there more you could do?

Help others to help yourself

We have found organizing some charity work a great way of helping your staff's mental health. Helping others in a crisis gives you some feeling of control, even when everything else feels out of control. Studies suggest that people have lower levels of the stress hormone cortisol when they do volunteer work and higher levels of feel-good chemicals like dopamine and serotonin (Bekkers et al., 2016; Sneed and Cohen, 2013).

Some of my team organized fundraising marathons during lockdown. For example, our Holiday Sweater Day brought people together virtually. We also raised money via social media for good causes and helped promote them via the company. It gave us a sense of purpose.

Charity work is not only good for your mental health, it can also deepen trust and loyalty with your stakeholders. Ed Templeton is a firm believer:

'During lockdown we worked with an organization that set up in the pandemic called Hospitality for Heroes. We had a team of volunteers, including our chefs and staff, but also regular customers, neighbours, industry friends, giving food donations and then cooking meals for NHS staff at the end of their shift.

'This kept the team busy, kept us thinking, kept us creative. And I think that helped us when we were able to open again at the end of June. Things were up and running. It wasn't having to walk into a dusty, empty building. It was a place that had actually been filled with people doing something good and creative.

'It was amazing because we had our customers side by side with our team cooking together and it was real community volunteering. I think they could see we're a business that has a heart. And it made good business sense because but it also had a really genuine social function. Over two and a half months we prepared around 10,000 meals.

'On top of that, our customer base thought, my God, even despite the horror, these guys are wearing their heart on their sleeve and they're rolling up their sleeves and getting on with it, and doing something that's genuinely purposeful. That matters. And that's what brands are all about now. And that will stand us in good stead for the long haul.'

Emily Arikian adds:

'One of the best things we did during Covid was to link up with an organization called Cards for Kids. I just invited the team to take 10, 20 minutes in the staff room and make a card.

'There are so many mental health benefits to colouring. It seems silly, but just unplugging for a second and drawing a card, relieving stress, improving brain function, focus, alleviating anxiety.

'Then we sent all the cards to the hospital and they were delivered to all the kids who had chronic illnesses. That's a really nice thing to do together and just give back and take a moment and pause collectively.

'So things like that, just making sure you're investing in your team and not forgetting that they're human. They're not robots.'

Looking after your team's mental health is another way of putting people first. A healthy, happy workforce will result in improved productivity and employee retention. In turn that can lead to happier customers and improved profits.

It will also be good for you as a leader, and it is also really important for you to look after your own wellbeing. You are no use to anyone if you are stressed or out of sorts, so let's now turn to how to protect *you* during a crisis.

The Flexible Method tools – Care for your team's mental health

▶ Set up a workplace mental health strategy
▶ Spot employees who are struggling
▶ Do something fun that encourages friendship and warmth at work
▶ Giving is purposeful and good for mental health

CHAPTER FOURTEEN

Mind your own health

Sarah Wait sat at her living room table in Kingston upon Thames, south-west London, chatting to her HR manager online about how her team were doing. She runs a forward-planning service at Onclusive, a leading media planning agency that provides insights into future trends which companies can then use to plan their future strategies. She founded and built this business over 20 years, so she has lived through plenty of crises.

During the Covid-19 pandemic she regularly checked in with her young team as they struggled to cope with working from home. One day, as the discussion was winding up, the HR manager asked: *'And how are YOU doing?'*

Sarah unexpectedly burst into tears. *'Evidently not as well as I thought,'* she eventually managed to reply. Cumulative pressures had been building up unnoticed for some time.

Selfless leaders like Sarah are often the last to worry about themselves. While this might sound noble, neglecting your own health during a long, intense period of working is not smart management. It can lead to poor decision-making and may harm your organization.

You are no use to anyone if you are tired, stressed and unwell. Looking after your own health is therefore critical.

I am happy to report Sarah recognized she needed to improve her self-care, actioned some changes and is in great shape again.

Give yourself a break

As a strong, calm leader you put your people first, stepped up your communication, upheld your values, adapted your business and reached out to your network. You kept a close eye on your team's mental health as you steered through the crisis.

All this will have made your business more resilient. But leaders often overlook one thing: the importance of *them* staying well!

Self-care is often one of the most overlooked tasks and can also be one of the most difficult to execute. But go to any business school now or look along the shelves of a good bookstore and you will notice a seismic shift – self-care has become one of the key qualities of a leader.

A crucial pillar of the Flexible Method is self-care. You need to take your wellbeing seriously and you need to commit to it.

Lonely at the top

Crises are especially tough on leaders. Navigating through uncertainty, dealing with heightened expectations and having to look after everyone else's mental health heaps extra stress on leaders. This was exacerbated during the Covid-19 pandemic when our social lives were severely restricted, removing this vital stress valve. I think some of us have been close to breaking down as a result.

Mental health services all over the world have been inundated with people seeking help. If you have felt bad, you are not alone.

At the best of times we can struggle to cope with the day-to-day stress of busy workloads. But dealing with the additional pressure of a crisis can push you over the edge.

During the Covid-19 pandemic psychotherapist Emily Arikian was providing online counselling:

'For me, it was really good for my own mental health to still feel useful, still feel like I'm giving back and being a support, but there was a period when I billed 144 sessions in a week, which is a really large number and was not healthy. It took a toll. So I tried to be self-aware, noticing I'm not sleeping, my diet's changed, or if I want to drink more or I'm just being bitchy to my family.

'I told them, "If you notice something about me, let me know." And then being receptive to that, not taking offence but saying, "Okay, thank you for letting me know that I'm acting different."'

Early warning signs

Things tend to get on top of you gradually so you don't notice. To stop this happening, recognize the warning signs early on. Look in the mirror and ask yourself if you are showing any of these telltale signs that things are becoming too much:

▶ More irritable than usual?
▶ Sleeping poorly?
▶ Lacking energy?
▶ Routine tasks leaving you overwhelmed?
▶ Pervasive feeling of anxiety/dread?
▶ Drinking too much?
▶ Comfort eating?

Any of this sounding familiar? If so, don't dismiss it as weakness or tell yourself that you don't have time to deal with it right now. Listen to your trusted inner circle – empower them to be honest with you. They might spot that you are getting stressed before you do, just as you might find it easier to recognize when a colleague is struggling.

The next step is to acknowledge you are under pressure. It happens to all of us. So please be kind to yourself. You deserve some TLC and you must learn how to give it to yourself.

What small thing can you do right now that will make you know that you care about yourself?

▶ Book a massage?
▶ Call a friend?
▶ Play a game with the kids?
▶ Walk the dog?
▶ Cook a meal for a loved one?
▶ Take a bath?
▶ Change into some comfortable clothes and pick up a novel?

Winning gold – the smart way

I often compare leaders to athletes. Our goal is to win gold medals. We need to prepare for races well in advance. The preparation starts with rest, then strategic planning, slowly building targeted exercises, healthy nutrition, sleep, mental preparation, increased exercise and then the Big Day. Sometimes we win gold! And then it is back to rest... and the cycle can start again.

You will not win a gold medal every time. And will not win many golds at all if all you do is slog, slog, slog.

I know it can feel incredibly counterintuitive to take time out, especially during a pressing crisis. But looking after your well-being is a skill that needs to be practised until it becomes a habit. Most of us simply need to up our game on self-care and we can do this within our day-to-day at work.

Where to start? Does your office look nice? Is the desk clear? When did you last buy yourself some flowers?

I strongly recommend you break each day into bite-size chunks. The macho culture of working solidly for hours on end is not fit for purpose. And you will never perform at your best. Less is more.

Lunch is not for wimps

I have learned over the years that taking breaks reaps unexpected rewards. It is almost like a universal law: if I am staring at something, willing it to happen, fretting over it, then it will inevitably delay, and maybe never even happen at all. But if I let go ... if I turn my back and go and do something completely different, that thing that was stuck often clicks into gear and takes off of its own accord. It is quite weird but it works.

Turning your back can be quite simple. When was the last time you went for a brisk walk in the middle of your work day or read a book for pleasure over lunchtime? In fact, when was the last time you took a proper lunch break and just chatted with your colleagues about nothing in particular? These are some of the things that make life joyful.

Working from home often means you carry on working long after you should have stopped. Be more disciplined about your hours. I strongly recommend that you set boundaries. Add regular breaks to your schedule and ring-fence time out.

It may now be time to ask your team to share your workload. Can you delegate more? I know they will be under tremendous pressure themselves and you are reluctant to dump more work on them, but there may be new initiatives you can postpone. Focus your time on areas that will have the biggest impact on your organization.

Have you ever advised struggling colleagues to work smarter not harder? If so, maybe it's time to practise what you preach.

Let's get physical

When you free up a little time, you can start replenishing your flagging energy. Exercise and diet are good places to start. Can you carve out time to exercise two or three times a week? The release of endorphins is well documented – exercise improves your mood. It can also change your perspective. I try to go to the gym twice a week and run or brisk walk at least once more. Sometimes it is a struggle.

These days you don't even have to leave the house to exercise, with a huge range of workouts or yoga classes available online. I have friends who have invested in all sorts of wonderful spinning machines and gadgets. Or you can join a gym, or a group in a local park. Start small and build.

When I went to study at the Saïd Business School at the University of Oxford a few years ago, we were invited to go running with our classmates every morning. I was up for it but had never been particularly interested in sport and unfortunately it was not rooted in my family upbringing either. So I had to start from scratch. Which meant literally walking for five minutes, then running for one. Walking for four minutes, then running for one. I was slow!

I did stick to the regime, with encouragement from some kindly coaches and my classmates, and after three weeks I was running with the group around Oxford every morning before breakfast. We even did laps where Roger Bannister broke the four-minute mile. Whenever I am flagging on a run now, I think of Oxford and it gives me that boost to finish. For the first time in my life, I came to love the feeling of waking up and exercising.

When I went to the grad school at Stanford in California a few years later, we did circuit training before breakfast. This included one-minute planks – where you raise yourself up on your elbows and hold firm like a plank. It is great for building your core strength. I thank that venerable institution for giving me many things, but possibly best of all a good plank.

When we are busy and stressed it's not only our business decisions that are affected, our dietary choices tend to go to hell too.

Bad habits

Do you fuel yourself with caffeine and sugar throughout the day? I don't need to tell you that this is not a great choice. I find it useful to have healthy snacks like fruit and nuts on hand. We are bombarded with ads for fast food, but ask yourself how long a healthy meal like scrambled eggs and avocado on toast takes. Minutes. And eating away from your desk will not only avoid crumbs in your keyboard, it will aid your digestion too.

I worked with a nutritionist for a few months and she got me thinking more mindfully about what I was eating and when. I thoroughly recommend getting some expert advice, or at least learning more about your eating habits and adapting them.

Many of us are dehydrated. I heard a doctor say that if you could do just one thing to stay healthy it should be to drink a glass of water with every meal. It works wonders at flushing out toxins. I try to drink two litres a day if possible.

And when you do eventually finish work, try not to habitually drink alcohol to unwind. I regularly go teetotal for a week or more at a time just to give my body a break. I don't drink that heavily usually, but a clear head and body after a detox is my favourite place to be.

With his chain of gyms closed during lockdown, John Grim found himself at home every day with his wife and their new baby:

'I found it incredibly tough being locked down. I probably drank more than I'd ever drunk. It financially just turned my life upside down. The goalposts were constantly being moved, with the government saying one thing then changing their mind. I was really bitter about it.'

Despite his anger and anxiety, John took some positive action: 'My wife and I trained in the garden every morning and enjoyed the sun. She lost a stone in weight. I got in super shape.'

As well as being a great stress burner, physical exercise is great for helping you sleep. Getting adequate sleep is not an ideal, nice-to-have; it is essential if you are to perform effectively. In a crisis leaders tend to work long hours and sleep sporadically. This will end up making you less and less effective.

We seem to be living in an age of endemic insomnia. Anxiety and depression are major causes of this. Do you check emails late at night? Please don't. In fact, unplug yourself from all screens for at least half an hour before you go to sleep. I switch off my phone and computers at night and put them somewhere safe. Not in the bedroom.

And if you really cannot sleep, then talk to your doctor. You must sleep to function. Without sleep, you are nothing.

Joy division

As well as your physical wellbeing, it is crucial you pay attention to your mental health. I know, here I go stating the obvious again, but sometimes we are so focused on complex, fast-changing situations in a crisis that we overlook the obvious.

I recommend you start to put more joy into your life. Joy comes from many places, including spending time with the people you love, small things like gardening or cooking or going for a walk, taking quality time to be in the present moment.

A change of scene can also be a reliable way to boost your sense of joyfulness. If you can't take a vacation, how about a weekend away? Leave your laptop at home and give yourself a digital detox. A radical thought.

Even while you are working, you should stop trying to always keep on top of the deluge of emails, messaging and news coming at you. Shut down some of that noise or it will drive you mad.

Some problems feel insoluble and you can fry your brain trying to figure out what to do. When your thoughts are going round and round without any good effect, this may be a time to turn off your conscious mind and let your thoughts drift. Going for a walk, swimming and cycling do the trick for me. Practising meditation is also effective.

Just parking a problem and sleeping on it can suddenly put things into perspective. If you are lucky, solutions can emerge in the morning.

If you are interested in working on improving your mental strength, then it is worth exploring mindfulness. There are some excellent books with CDs you can buy and courses all over the world. I have done a course at the Oxford Mindfulness Centre, which lasted for six evenings over six weeks. It helped me hone the technique of getting centred in a storm and seeing changing moods as weather patterns that come and go. It is a very useful tool which you can apply in your day-to-day.

I also recommend you see a professional therapist if there are stresses in your life that are worrying you. Most things can be overcome with a little help.

This is not a last resort. In fact, it can be a very useful tool for helping you stay well and strong long term. A therapist can offer you various methods for coping, relaxing and managing stress. Consulting a professional to help you with your thinking is some-thing I support (take a look at books on cognitive behavioural therapy, for example).

I've said it before but helping others can lift your mood and be good for your mental health. You never have to look too hard to find someone in a more difficult situation than yourself. Reach-ing out to help them is a kind and purposeful thing to do, plus it boosts your self-esteem and puts your problems into perspective.

I find that talking to close friends and family is good for the soul. They are a source of strength which you should regularly tap into.

Make time for the people who are closest to you. They will help refill your drained emotional energy. When was the last time you met up with a friend who makes you laugh? Again, building more of this joy into your life will make you happier and a better leader.

Just as you need to stop fuelling your body with toxic sub-stances and your mind with toxic thoughts, are you in toxic rela-tionships that drain your energy and make you stressed? If so, set boundaries. Consider parking the relationship for a while or even block them out. Especially in a crisis you need positive, support-ive people around you.

My advice is, if you know it makes sense, don't wait until 'the time is right' before taking action to help yourself. The time is now. If you wait until things are calmer, the problems may get worse.

Overwhelm

After the worst of the crisis is over, it is likely you will feel a huge sense of relief. It will be time to rest and recuperate. But beware, you may also be caught out by an unexpected aftershock – overwhelm.

After so many hours, weeks, days, even months of intense noise, pressure, conflicts and emotions, you may feel the need to let off steam and celebrate. This is important and will be good for you. In small doses.

I recommend not overdoing it. It may be tempting to go out and party, connect with every single one of your family and friends, organize a dozen events, travel the country or take flights all over the world. But just be careful not to overwhelm your senses. Remember, your entire body, mind and spirit have been through the wringer. Go gently as you come through the crisis and out the other side. Overwhelm is a real possibility.

If you do get overwhelmed, there are plenty of things you can do to ease the pressure:

▶ Reduce your commitments, including social ones.
▶ Stay in one place.
▶ Reduce travel.
▶ Have a digital detox.
▶ Keep things simple – focus on close family and friends.
▶ Do small things like cook, walk the dog, water the garden or plant a window box.
▶ Eat well and sleep.

It will pass. And if it doesn't, then deploy your usual self-care tools and even consult some professional help if needed. Your wise self will know what to do.

Bright side of life

Caring for yourself can boost your productivity, memory, focus, creativity, empathy and decision-making – in other words, your overall effectiveness as a leader. These benefits are backed up by clear research data.

I hope you have found that some ideas in this chapter help you to feel a sense of optimism and hope. This is very important. Trying to insert more joyful moments into your life will make you happier and stronger. It will also make you a better leader.

Making the time for actions that will help you is a good investment for the future and you will reap the dividends when the crisis has passed.

Looking after yourself is a key part of the Flexible Method.

So, congratulations will now be in order. The worst is over. You have steered your organization through the crisis with your values guiding you, new allies at your side and all the help you are entitled to. You adapted your business, supercharging your creativity to find new markets with impressive ingenuity.

You will be battered and bruised, but caring for your own and your team's wellbeing will mitigate the stresses as you gradually emerge from the dark days.

Now is no time to rest on your laurels, though. Crises contain big opportunities that not only can help you to recover but can also rapidly accelerate your progress. This is an exciting prospect that we turn to next.

The Flexible Method tools – Mind your own health

▶ Investing in your health is crucial
▶ Take time out
▶ Recognize the warning signs of cumulative stress
▶ Listen to supportive people around you
▶ Cultivate more joy in your life
▶ Block out toxic relationships
▶ Consult the experts if you need to

PART 4

Emerging from a crisis: new horizons

CHAPTER FIFTEEN

Set your future course

Twelve months into Covid-19 we faced a sliding-doors moment at Argonon: hunker down and survive the storm or adjust our sails and plot a new course?

Staying careful with our cash and spending was the safe bet in such uncertain waters, but we chose to be confident in the strength of the market and our own abilities. We embarked on a strategy for growth.

I knew it was ambitious and it raised a few eyebrows, but it gave us a common purpose and was founded in the opportunities we saw in the post-crisis landscape. We call it the Great Reset and we see evidence of this around the world.

Our first strategic decision was to invest in the branded content firm Nemorin. As commercial channels struggled with long-term decline in traditional advertising, we saw an opportunity with branded content as a new alternative revenue stream. This means that brands like Coca-Cola, Red Bull or Nike fund programming content instead of relying on commissions from TV networks.

Laura Bessell, Argonon COO, recalls:

'The pandemic meant that there were a lot of smaller businesses out there looking to team up with new partners to reduce their

exposure to risk. When you think another disaster could happen, being part of a bigger infrastructure suddenly becomes more attractive as smaller operators have less appetite to fly solo.

'In turn, bigger companies were looking to further diversify their businesses with new income streams.'

We also grew our Los Angeles hub, where the big content players are headquartered. We launched a new joint venture with a very exciting producer who was looking to spread his wings with a smart international backer.

Keep an eye out for talent, as well. Crises have a habit of throwing everybody's thinking up in the air. In my industry, we saw a lot of people taking stock. Some left the industry altogether during Covid as they changed priorities and chose to spend more time with the kids or move from the big city to the country.

Many others realized that they had not been happy in their current work situation. They felt frustrated, held back, undervalued or underpaid. This is an opportunity for employers and employees to find a better future.

We spotted a lot of exciting TV production talent in the US and the UK who were on the move and looking for a more supportive and enlightened work environment. Some were looking for a punchier deal. We set ourselves a budget and a strategic plan and went out of our way to attract this talent into our group. We have successfully grown our team as a result. This has opened new doors for us as they bring expertise and clients who were previously unavailable to us.

This expansionist strategy has been validated. Argonon is now the fastest growing super indie in the UK, with 50 per cent year-on-year growth and revenues considerably up on pre-Covid levels. We achieved this by employing the Flexible Method: putting people first, leading with calm purpose, thinking flexibly, adapting, then executing decisions with radical determination.

As you begin to emerge from a crisis, this is the time to plan your future course. It could lead to permanent changes in your business.

If you successfully adapted your organization in a crisis, you should be well placed to emerge more resilient to shocks. Your business model innovations may have increased your competitive edge. Even if the crisis has weakened your competitive position, you can still absorb lessons and take bold action to make up for lost ground.

A crisis often creates a sea change in people's behaviour that creates opportunities. As a leader, I urge you to embrace the change and use this time purposefully.

Horizon scanning

The first thing you need to do as you begin to emerge from a crisis is assess what has changed in the new norm. The disruption of the crisis may have resulted in new areas to explore while others are less attractive now. Customers may have changed their behaviour, for example turning away from in-store retail and switching to online purchasing.

Use data to carefully identify which changes in customer behaviour are likely to be permanent. Flexible, open-minded thinking is key to working out what is happening in your traditional areas. Be prepared for surprises.

The 9/11 attacks changed attitudes about privacy and security, resulting in permanently higher levels of screening and surveillance. Covid-19 accelerated e-commerce. Gym owners Rob and John Grim now offer online PT sessions for executives working from home, for example. Restaurants have moved to home delivery, while retail banks are among many organizations that are closing branches to shift online, with staff working from home.

There may also be short-term changes you can exploit. Your competitors and customers can give you clues. Who is doing well in the new landscape? What areas are they looking at?

The key to success at this stage is to raise your eyes from day-to-day problems and look six months ahead.

In LA, rather than going for a knee-jerk reaction to current demands during Covid, Lindsay Schwartz, Chief Creative Officer at Leopard USA, was scanning the post-crisis horizon:

'When Covid first started everyone was clamouring for Zoom-based shows and were trying to figure out what the next Zoom show would be. I thought we were going to get so sick of these types of shows, so creating new business in that space didn't seem like the right way to go. And in fact everyone quickly said, we don't want another Zoom show, we don't want to see a mask, we don't want to talk about Covid.

'Someone pitched us a Zoom-based show that had a deal at the Oprah Winfrey Network. And we ended up taking that idea and thinking, how can we turn that into something bigger and different that people will want to buy in three to six months? So we completely reformatted it into a super-fresh regular show, not a Zoom-based show. And we ended up selling it to Hulu.

'Strategy is very circumstantially based. There are no hard and fast rules. And I think that's where people get into problems, when they say, this is the way things are, this is how we do things and that's it. If anyone says that you know they're a dinosaur and they're not going to get anywhere because you constantly have to re-evaluate, especially in a creative space. The rules you thought were applicable yesterday are not going to be applicable tomorrow. It's about really being flexible.

'Creatively, I think the immediate outcome of the pandemic is more aspirational programming. We use television as escape. My number one example is House Hunters International *because you*

watch it for 22 minutes and you've escaped to a different location without getting on a plane. Without exposing yourself to Covid or any other disease.'

Lindsay's flexible mindset and ability to think beyond the immediate horizon are big assets to us.

Brave new world

One you have figured out the potential ramifications of the new landscape, you must adapt your business model to respond. Identify specific products and services that will be in demand or opportunities that will most likely grow as a result.

Crises will probably involve the accelerated adoption of technology, which means you now offer new digital products and services. This may require new partnerships. Perhaps you can continue with partners that you collaborated with during the crisis, but you may need to develop new ones from your sector and beyond to thrive in this new post-crisis landscape.

Retail is one sector that defied the doom-mongers and successfully reinvented itself during Covid. Many thought the shock to the system would destroy its stores, but it actually accelerated much-needed change. Some stores did close for good, of course, but overall the sector has benefited in the long term from big investments in technology. US shoppers stuck at home for months accumulated cash which they spent online like never before. Retailers created the omnichannel concept, combining bricks-and-mortar stores and the internet. Customers could order online and pick up in-store, for example. Online grocery deliveries were speeded up thanks to innovations in warehouse robotics and electronic shelf tags.

In the US, Best Buy was among the chains that established curbside pickup systems during the pandemic. Target's shopping app even allows drive-up customers to choose exactly where bags are placed in their car.

In Britain, the department store chain Marks & Spencer, which had been struggling for years, used the pandemic to speed up its transformation. It shut struggling branches and partnered with the online grocery service Ocado, boosting its stock by 60 per cent and returning healthy profits.

Splash the cash...

The third step to take as you emerge from a crisis is to boldly invest where appropriate. Great disruption can create great opportunities. The management consulting company McKinsey found that companies that acted fast and invested strongly ahead of the recovery from the Credit Crunch increased their EBITDA by 10 per cent, while their industry peers lost nearly 15 per cent (McKinsey, 2015).

You have been through the pain. Now is precisely the time to shake off the cautionary approach you were forced to adopt during the crisis and take swift, bold action. During the crisis, you had to carefully protect your cash. That time is over. If you responded rapidly to the challenges, don't take your foot off the gas now as things start to recover. Remember, you must speculate to accumulate, and a post-crisis world is ripe with promise.

Despite struggling to survive during the pandemic, Ed Templeton's hospitality business seized an opportunity to expand, renting three townhouses for a competitive rent on Charlotte Street in a prime restaurant area of central London.

'Normally you'd be paying a premium in excess of half a million pounds to rent that building, and then everything else involved. So this is a unique opportunity post-Covid, to actually take on a building that's ten times better than anything we would've ever been able to get our hands on before. I spoke to some very wise business heads at the time, who said, "You've got to do it."

'Part of the reason we attracted a really good team and kept them was saying, "Look, when we move from here we're going to open this amazing new place." I think the confidence of actually surviving, financially, made us a better, stronger business.'

...but don't rush in

That said, you need to move circumspectly. Most crises don't end overnight. High levels of uncertainty are likely to persist and you must not call time on a crisis prematurely. It is important to watch out for aftershocks, so stay alert and monitor the evolving situation. The crisis may be over but, like a movie monster or villain, they have a nasty tendency to resurface just when you think you are in the clear.

Ideally, though, you will move boldly and take a few well-considered risks while your competitors are still hanging back, nervously scanning the horizon.

A sensible strategy is to take a portfolio approach to investment. Explore multiple opportunities as you move forward. For example, you may choose to take a minority stake in a company with an option to increase it later. While diversifying your portfolios, most of your spending should ideally, of course, be in higher-growth sectors.

Setting a new course

As the crisis is abating you should announce to your team that your organization will shift from immediate operational survival needs to focus on longer-term strategies. When you communicate with your team as you emerge from a crisis, paint an inspiring picture of the direction you want your organization to take and explain how they and your customers will benefit.

There may be a psychological tendency to default to old habits, but as a leader you must challenge this if you are to prosper in the new landscape. It's time to cast off the shackles.

One thing you certainly shouldn't cast away after the crisis are the closer connections to your customers and your team. You put people first during the crisis and led honestly and empathetically. Changing this now would damage the trust people invested in you and which you will have to draw on when the next crisis comes.

Your team have been through the mill and will need a rest – and I imagine you may need one too after taking on board the huge range of suggestions in this book – so as we approach the final chapter of this journey, let's now turn to the best ways of managing this.

The Flexible Method tools – Set your future course

▶ Assess the post-crisis landscape
▶ Identify new opportunities
▶ Develop new partnerships if required
▶ Proceed boldly
▶ Monitor the evolving situation
▶ If apt, invest to grow

CHAPTER SIXTEEN

Rest, reward, review

Whoa there, tiger!

As the craziness of Covid receded my team were fired up about new opportunities. Some were still running on adrenalin, but I could see the crisis had taken its toll. A leader's job is to show the way and right now our team needed to rest.

I found it very important to schedule some time out and I encouraged my team to do the same. This trickled down through our organization. As more and more of our team took a break, I could see and feel the tension dissipating.

If you have followed the Flexible Method there will most likely be exciting opportunities for you in the post-crisis landscape. While it might be tempting to push your team on to exploit these opportunities, I would advise taking a counterintuitive step and pressing the pause button in this respect.

I urge you to take time out as you emerge from a crisis and encourage your team to let go for a bit to recharge batteries. They will need to regain their work–life balance. The stress and anxiety of the crisis will have used up their reserves. Now is the time to replenish them.

Depending on the crisis, your team may have suffered trauma and grief also. This needs to be acknowledged and taken into account. You may even have to insist on this with some members of your team. They are going to need all their energy in the months to come. Time out is especially important for creative minds.

Gratitude

Constantly expressing positive feedback to your employees is important, but after a crisis it is essential. Every one of your team will have made sacrifices and they need to hear that their dedication is recognized and that it made a difference. Showcase great work across your business, highlighting what and *how* employees are achieving it. This is also a way of exemplifying new behaviours that contribute to your organization's success.

It is not only the right thing to do as an empathetic leader, a little gratitude yields big returns in productivity and resilience.

When you finally emerge from the crisis, I would encourage you to bring everyone together and publicly share your appreciation of the team as a whole and of individuals, especially those who tend to remain out of the spotlight. Praise these unsung heroes.

Expressing thanks is all the more important when staff are working remotely. It is easy to overlook people when they are not physically present. A culture of recognition and appreciation will cascade these positive expressions of thankfulness and foster teamwork as people who have received thankfulness are in turn more generous and helpful to others.

I'm sure you will have experienced how corrosive it is to work for an organization where the staff feel overworked, underappreciated and isolated. Appreciation and recognition go a long way to avoid this.

Psychological research shows that gratitude is also good for your own health and wellbeing, so expressing it is a real win-win and it is something that you should continue in a timely and authentic way long after a crisis has passed (Ackerman, 2017).

Reward

Your gratitude for your team's work during the crisis should also be followed up with tangible rewards. These rewards can take many forms – cash, opportunities for development, celebrations.

Laura Bessell, Argonon COO, sums up the company's view:

'After the initial pandemic we did reward staff. We looked at overtime and at those people that had really gone above and beyond – they had either cut their hours and then continued to work similar hours as when they were on a full-time salary, or they'd continually work weekends and late nights. We paid bonuses to reward them for what they had done.

'Where people have really demonstrated their leadership qualities, we've given them quite significant pay rises.

'With other staff, especially those with young kids, we negotiated a much more flexible working pattern. So there are different kinds of rewards as part of a package.'

Tobias Simons is a Head of Reward for a Fortune 500 multi-national which operates in over 100 countries.

In addition to standard salary practice, Tobias mentions that more and more organizations are looking at how to be 'flexible' in the way they reward staff – this could be through flexible benefits to flexible working patterns. What is becoming increasingly important though is that people want to be able to customize their reward package towards their individual needs. Tobias feels that this way of rewarding staff will become more commonplace after the Covid pandemic: 'The world has changed and it is unlikely to change back. This was a seismic shift and one that I think needed to happen. Organizations have long spoken about wellbeing and work–life balances, but not really done much about it in terms of change. The Pandemic in many ways has made that shift and people are not prepared to go back.'

'The world has changed and it won't change back. This was a seismic shift and one I think that needed to happen. When you bleat on about wellbeing and work–life balances, as we have done for many years, nobody's really done anything about it. The pandemic has actually made that shift and people are not prepared to go back.

'This is part of what's causing the "great resignation" at the moment because so many people have said, "I'm not prepared to go back to what I was doing before. I've had this road to Damascus moment where I've realized that my life is more important, and the way that I balance my life is more important than selling my soul to the company."

'As an employer, if you are looking to attract and retain talent, if you're not offering flexible hours, flexible working arrangements, whether that be working from the office X number of days a week or not, you won't get people accepting your job offers, no matter how much you are putting into the salary piece.

'Personally, I think it's a good thing because productivity has gone up massively across most organizations. The conversation around the four-day week has started picking up again because we are seeing that people can do a lot more with a lot less time as they are more focused on what they are doing and better able to manage their time (on both work and personal demands) through flexible working arrangements.

'That's not to say the office environment isn't a good thing, too. You need that. You need integration. It's a balance between the *two, but offering that flexibility is going to be a very important key reward aspect for any employer if they want to be competitive going forwards.'*

We will not see a return to the way things were. Change, thanks to the pandemic, is permanent. To be honest, it brings many benefits. Individual and personalized rewards, tailor-made to each employee, are also going to be effective. This is a key component of the Flexible Method.

Tobias says:

'You can get more traction with smaller, more meaningful things: a note to say, "That was a really great piece of work you did on that project. Thank you. Here's a voucher for a hundred dollars", whatever it may be. "Take your family out for a meal this evening to celebrate." That will have a lot more impact.'

Recognition is an integral component of reward.

'We have really successful recognition programmes where there's no tacit reward attached to it, and actually, that is where people get called out in meetings, get praised and are highlighted for the good work that they do. Likewise, people get recognition through the fact that they are then asked to go on to projects that are not necessarily related to their specific work, as a part of a reward saying, "You did so well on this job, we'd love you to get involved in this project."'

I love this. I love the fact that this particular crisis, so traumatic in so many ways. has forced us to evaluate and it's forcing us to do things differently. And it's getting us, as employers, to come up with very innovative, new, holistic ways of attracting people. And it's changing us for the better, frankly.

It's not even that employers have to come up with stuff; they just have to listen to what their people want and then think about how to include this in a structure that can work from both the employer and the employee perspective. And the more an employer does that, the easier they will find it to hold on to good people because they will be happy in their jobs.

On 23 December 2021, Elen Maggs's oven broke down. Thinking she was going to be without a cooker over Christmas, she shared news of the disaster with colleagues at the British retailer Timpson on their WhatsApp group. Without her knowledge, they called Timpson's Director of Happiness. A few days later, a new oven was delivered straight to her kitchen – paid for by the company.

Janet Leighton, Timpson's Director of Happiness, told *The Guardian* newspaper that these personal touches are not 'nice-to-haves' but are rooted in evidence-based, positive psychological research that yields concrete results. According to her, it makes commercial sense as employees are calm, relaxed and hardworking when they feel they are getting support and care. They are also more considerate to one another and customers.

The role is becoming increasingly high-profile. In 2022, Clifford Chance, one of London's oldest City law firms, proposed a new approach and appointed a Chief Happiness Officer to ensure staff enjoy 'the most vibrant, happy and uplifting place to work in the world'.

Happiness officers are tasked to create a 360-degree environment that combines salary, working hours, values and culture in a totally flexible new way. I see this as a major advance.

Many of us do not have the budget to create a dedicated role such as this, but at Argonon, for example, we have shared the responsibility for happiness around a number of our staff, from HR to my PA. They do a lot of listening to staff, are constantly proposing new ideas for us to bring into the group. It really is a 360 holistic approach, making certain our people know they are valued.

Tobias says:

'Environment, sustainability and governance (ESG) are now starting to play into all aspects of company life including rewards. These could be linked to carbon-reduction targets, as employees are interested in sustainability and are asking about it as part of the employee value proposition.

'I think you're seeing this morphing of employers becoming much more important to people as to what does my employer stand for, how do they treat people, how do they treat the environment and how do they treat me?'

As leaders we will miss out on the best talent in the future if we do not act now to reflect the change in expectations.

Celebrate

At Argonon, we have made group celebrations a way of life. It costs time and money to organize parties, of course, but it is worth every penny.

We throw parties twice a year most years and invite great DJs to come and play. I want to get everybody dancing until late. It is always such fun to mix all of our teams together with a few drinks and a very relaxed party atmosphere. We invite some friends to add to the mix and just a few of our more easy-going clients.

Our teams love to dress up, so we've often had a theme – *Dallas* vs *Dynasty* was a particularly good night.

Review

Let's turn to the third R. Now is also the time to review the key lessons hard won from the crisis.

- ▶ What did you do best?
- ▶ Where did you struggle?
- ▶ Can you simplify or improve your organization?
- ▶ What did you lack?
- ▶ What are the key threats you now face?
- ▶ Is there anything we learn from our competitors?

As we are so closely involved with our own businesses, we need to ensure our review is objective and analytical so that we derive useful lessons from the crisis. Our team should also be involved.

Looking back at the pandemic, we did some things really well at Argonon which we have talked about in the previous chapters.

Susie Field, former General Manager, Argonon, offers her view:

'I think crises are good for business. You need to have some kind of change every few years, otherwise things drift or people become complacent. I think it's really healthy. Some people are just really stuck and you can't be stuck in a creative business like this. You've got to be out there. You've got to get up from your desk and get outside and get ideas and work with different people.'

In some ways we have come back to the beginning of the process of the Flexible Method: preparing for the next crisis. But this doesn't mean just going back to the beginning and waiting for all the hardship and horror of a major crisis to start all over again.

I believe that if you follow the Flexible Method, you will emerge stronger and more resilient to shocks. I don't believe this out of blind optimism, this has been my experience of several crises and also of the businesses and organizations that have shared their stories with me in this book.

All of us suffered during the pandemic, which almost destroyed our livelihoods. But all of us have emerged stronger. Ed Templeton, restaurant owner, agrees with this:

'I think one of the principal positives to come out of Covid is having a leaner team that has adaptability woven into the fabric of who they are.

'It's amazing how quickly you can let silos build up within your own organization, right in front of your eyes, without fully realizing how damaging that can be. And I think reversing those effects is one of the real positives that came out of the pandemic.

'Our biggest learnings are ensuring that as an organization you're set up to be adaptable and flexible. And that you hire people who have those qualities.

'Being smarter and more dynamic about how we structure the business, that's been a huge lesson. The numbers are there. They tell you a story. I feel vindicated about belief in the team.'

Derek McLean, Executive Producer on *The Masked Singer* at our label Bandicoot Scotland, offers his view:

'The thing I've learned from Covid is that you get to know your people a lot quicker. So you've got to have a much sounder judgement in terms of people and teambuilding. The usefulness of everyone is so important in an organization. And you realize that everyone must contribute.

'I really did see it in terms of a war effort. And what I've realized is that it is as important to build the peace as it is to win the war. You learn these lessons in these crises and you don't put them away in a box when you're finished. You don't just think, that's over now, let's get back to where we were. The world shouldn't go back to where it was and we shouldn't go back to the people we were. You've got to keep moving forwards.'

Gym owners John and Rob Grim are equally positive. Rob says:

'I'm hopeful that we are gonna come through this stronger. And part of the reason is that our clients know we genuinely care about them. I think it's deepened relationships, actually. Having come through this together, there's a sense that it's created loyalty.'

John agrees with him:

'Yes, it has. The problem we've got with business is that a lot of the clients really get attached to their trainer, which is fantastic. So we must keep looking after our trainers, as we do. We've got some really long-standing trainers: some have been with us 10 or 14 years. So it's not just talk. We look after people and they look after us.

'We treat them with respect and then reward them for good work and appreciate them for someone doing little things.

'There are plenty of positives from the pandemic. The first year of my daughter growing up. Yeah. It was pretty magic. That summer was awesome.'

Fiona Allan, former CEO, Birmingham Hippodrome and now CEO, Opera Australia, has this to say:

'These painful experiences inform you, don't they? Then we have our wounds but nonetheless thanks to them we've learned so much

and you have skills and also you come out of it thinking, how has this changed the organization and our way of working together?

'For us it is about being open and far more flexible in terms of the way people work, with people working hybrid, being much more digitally aware. We could have been doing all of this stuff five or seven years ago but we weren't because we didn't have to.

'The digital acceleration has opened our eyes to using ways of doing things and we now have our eyes open to more interesting ways of looking at the world. What gives me great joy is how far we've moved on from where we were six years ago, and the pandemic has helped accelerate the development of our values. We are such a different place – so much more forward thinking, so much more inclusive, our minds so much broader, so I think yes, the pandemic has helped with that.'

Wrapping up

Thank you for coming on this journey with me. I appreciate your time. I know how busy you are.

I wrote this book to share some of our learnings at Argonon and the many extraordinary life-changing decisions and actions taken by my peers and colleagues across the planet, in many different industries, in multiple different crises. Truly it is a magnificent effort, painful for sure, but also transformative.

By summing up these many learnings as the Flexible Method, I have attempted to give you a set of ideas, thoughts and actions to help you when the next crisis hits. I have also sought to demonstrate that by putting your people first, taking a humble, listening stance, offering calm, purposeful leadership, being willing to pivot and then pursuing your decisions with radical determination, you will come out on top.

I know there are many more challenges ahead but together we will find a way.

I am certain that if you adopt the Flexible Method, you will come out the other side of any crisis a better leader and a more resilient organization.

Let's be hopeful about the future. I am optimistic about what comes next and look forward to sharing the coming journey with you.

The Flexible Method tools – Rest, reward, review

▶ Give your exhausted team a break
▶ Thank them
▶ Reward them for their tireless work and dedication
▶ Review what went right and what you can do better next time
▶ Commit to applying the lessons learned
▶ And then get back to prepare…

References

Ackerman, C. E. (2017) Benefits of gratitude: 28+ surprising research findings, https://positivepsychology.com/benefits-gratitude-research-questions/#:~:text=Results%20from%20this%20study%20showed, participants%20in%20the%20other%20groups

Ashlock, A. (2011) A reluctant 9/11 hero looks back, www.wbur.org/hereandnow/2011/09/09/benfante-reluctant-hero

BBC (2020) George Floyd: What happened in the final moments of his life, www.bbc.co.uk/news/world-us-canada-52861726

Bekkers, R., Konrath, S. H. and Smith, D. H. (2016) Physiological correlates of volunteering, https://core.ac.uk/outputs/81634020

Berman, M. and Thurkow, T. (2020) Covid-19 creates a moment of truth for corporate culture, www.bain.com/insights/covid-19-creates-a-moment-of-truth-for-corporate-culture/

Cholteeva, Y. (2022) Two-thirds of workers would not share mental health problems with their employer, poll finds, www.peoplemanagement. co.uk/article/1755631/two-thirds-workers-not-share-mental-health-problems-employer-poll-finds

Gardner, H. K. and Matviak, I. (2020) 7 strategies for promoting collaboration in a crisis, https://hbr.org/2020/07/7-strategies-for-promoting-collaboration-in-a-crisis

Gates, B. (2015) The next outbreak? We're not ready, www.youtube.com/watch?v=6Af6b_wyiwI

Gold, E. and Block, Z. (2011) *9.11.01*. Brown Alumni Magazine. https://www.brownalumnimagazine.com/articles/2011-09-08/91101

Hill, A. (2022) *'Commercial no-brainer': Why the role of happiness officer is taking off*. The Guardian. https://www.theguardian.com/lifeandstyle/2022/feb/25/commercial-no-brainer-why-role-of-happiness-officer-is-taking-off

HSE (2021) Work-related stress, anxiety or depression statistics in Great Britain, 2021, www.hse.gov.uk/statistics/causdis/stress.pdf

Kanter, R. M. (2010) BP's Tony Hayward and the failure of leadership accountability, *Harvard Business Review*. https://hbr.org/2010/06/bps-tony-hayward-and-the-failu

Lelliott, P. and Tulloch, S. (2008) Mental health and work, www.gov.uk/government/uploads/system/uploads/attachment_data/file/212266/hwwb-mental-health-and-work.pdf

McKinsey (2015) McKinsey on finance, www.mckinsey.com/~/media/McKinsey/Business%20Functions/Strategy%20and%20Corporate%20Finance/Our%20Insights/McKinsey%20on%20Finance%20Number%2056/MoF56%20Full%20Issue.ashx

Rice, D. and Dastagir, A. E. (2013) https://eu.usatoday.com/story/news/nation/2013/10/29/sandy-anniversary-facts-devastation/3305985/

Sneed, R. S. and Cohen, S. (2013) A prospective study of volunteerism and hypertension risk in older adults. *Psychology and Aging*, 28(2), 578–586, https://doi.org/10.1037/a0032718

Sridhar, D. (2022) *Preventable: How a pandemic changed the world & how to stop the next one*, Penguin Books

The de Bono Group (n.d.), Six Thinking Hats. https://www.debonogroup.com/services/core-programs/six-thinking-hats/

Twitter (2020) Vote for respect. Vote for decency. Vote for truth. Vote for leadership. https://twitter.com/joebiden/status/1323228219127046144

Walter, E. (2014) In business your reputation is the only currency that matters, www.forbes.com/sites/ekaterinawalter/2014/07/16/in-business-your-reputation-is-the-only-currency-that-matters/?sh=7e60d38e369e

Wikipedia (nd) Hurricane Katrina, https://en.wikipedia.org/wiki/Hurricane_Katrina

WordStream (nd) www.wordstream.com/about-us

Acknowledgements

Thank you to my publisher Holly Bennion for believing in this book and in me. You encouraged me to reach upwards with your expansive thinking.

Thank you to the talented team at Nicholas Brealey for your creativity and meticulous attention to detail - Meaghan Lim, Antonia Maxwell and the design team.

Thank you to my literary agent Nick Walters for your lateral thinking and calm purpose. Thank you also to my uber-agent David Luxton for giving me a first listen on this project and a steer on how to make it happen.

Thank you to Andy Sillett for your thoughtful editorial and strategic thinking, Rich Turner for your perspicacious editing, Lalit Johri and Seth Sherman for your wise observations and Angelica Reni, Tiffeny Seaford and Elle Diamond for your research.

Thank you to all my contributors who kindly told me your stories. I was inspired and moved by them all. Congratulations on leading the way so resolutely through the storms and coming out on top.

Alex Bellow
Andy Sillett
David Butcher
David Chikwe
David Holt

The Flexible Method

Davina McCall

Derek McLean

Ed Templeton

Emily Arikian

Fiona Allan

Georgia and Harry Maguire

Henry Scott

Janet Archer

Jenny King

Joey Attawia

John Grim

Kristian Smith

La'Ron Hines

Laura Bessell

Lee Gunn

Lindsay Schwartz

Liz Layton

Matt Orr

Michael Douglas

Neil Garfinkel

Nick Godwin

Rob Grim

Said Said

Sarah Wait

Shirley Escott

Susie Field

Tobias Simons

Tony Stanton

Thank you my team at Argonon who made this journey possible. I hope we will enjoy many more years together. Strength to your arms!

And thank you to my partner Joey – none of this would exist without your brilliance, insight, energy, kindness and compassion. And holding up the mirror. Onwards.

Would you like your people to read this book?

If you would like to discuss how you could bring these ideas to your team, we would love to hear from you. Our titles are available at competitive discounts when purchased in bulk across both physical and digital formats. We can offer bespoke editions featuring corporate logos, customized covers, or letters from company directors in the front matter can also be created in line with your special requirements.

We work closely with leading experts and organizations to bring forward-thinking ideas to a global audience. Our books are designed to help you be more successful in work and life.

For further information, or to request a catalogue, please contact: **business@johnmurrays.co.uk**
sales-US@nicholasbrealey.com (North America only)

Nicholas Brealey Publishing is an imprint of John Murray Press.